Recipes from
Miss Daisy's

25th Anniversary Edition

Recipes from
Miss Daisy's

Daisy King

Cumberland House
Nashville, Tennessee

Published by
Cumberland House Publishing
431 Harding Industrial Drive
Nashville, Tennessee 37211

Previous editions of this book were published in 1978 by Miss Daisy's
Tearoom, Franklin, Tennessee, and in 1985 by Rutledge Hill Press,
Nashville, Tennessee.

Cover design: Harriette Bateman

Library of Congress Cataloging-in-Publication Data
King, Daisy, 1945–
  Recipes from Miss Daisy's / Daisy King.– 25th Anniversary ed.
    p. cm.
  ISBN 1-58182-368-1 (comb-bound : alk. paper)
  1. Cookery, American—Southern style. 2. Cookery—Tennessee. 3. Miss
Daisy's Tearoom (Nashville, Tenn.) I. Title.
  TX715.2.S68K56 2003
  641.5975—dc21

                                                    2003011247

Printed in Canada
1 2 3 4 5 6 7—09 08 07 06 05 04 03

Miss Daisy's Tearoom dedicates this cookbook to our guests and friends who supported the Tearoom, inspired our aims, challenged our energies, and, lastly, purchased this book. We hope our efforts inspire you to repeat a favorite meal at home.

Contents

Introduction   3

Luncheon at the Tearoom   7

Miss Daisy at Home   45

Sunday Down South   95

Special Days at the Restaurant   121

Index   145

Recipes from
Miss Daisy's

Introduction

Marilyn Lehew and I opened Miss Daisy's Tearoom in 1974. Our guests began requesting the recipes right away and continued to do so. Thus in 1978, twenty-five years ago, we shared our joy of cooking in this cookbook with recipes from Brunches, Lunches, Teas, and Dinners.

Back then our recipes were as natural as could be. We used real butter and fresh herbs, made our sauces from scratch, and baked our own breads and desserts. They are still as timeless today.

Helen Corbitt, the author of many cookbooks and the operator for many years of the Zodiac Room (the restaurant in Nieman Marcus stores), was a mentor for the original menu at Miss Daisy's. She insisted I use her Creamed Chicken recipe. Marilyn Lehew continues to serve the recipe at her own restaurant, The Stoveworks at The Factory in Franklin, Tennessee.

I want to reflect some of the nostalgia of our Miss Daisy beginnings for those readers who are using the recipes for the first time. We began with a very domestic kitchen that was painted yellow, like the one in my own house, and had a non-commercial dishwasher, also like the one in my own house! Quickly, that dishwashing method changed because we found that the number of guests we had—and the number of dirty plates to wash—greatly exceeded our expectations. The

Tearoom was housed in a beautiful turn-of-the-century house across from the Carter House in Franklin. The Carter House still stands and is one of Franklin's Historical Homes.

As guests visited Miss Daisy's, some felt so at home they would create their own parking spaces and seat themselves without consulting the hostess. They would bring their corporate checkbooks to pay three-dollar lunch tabs. But most of all they had fun and loved the food. I could fill pages dropping names of luminaries who dined at Miss Daisy's, but we saw all our guests as special people, and as they finished a meal and departed they became Tearoom friends.

I have written many cookbooks since this one, but none has received more attention than this one, widely known as "The Little Yellow Cookbook." When people meet me and recognize the name, they immediately tell me their favorite Miss Daisy's story and who they have served our recipes to—and how much they have been enjoyed. After we sold over a half million copies of this "Little Yellow Cookbook," we stopped counting!

* * *

I would like to pay tribute to our late friend, Judy Wheeler, who was the original editor of this book. Judy wanted me to write a cookbook so much that she gave her time and talents in 1978 to help this work become a reality. Mary Sanford is our present editor, and we thank her for helping make this edition possible.

I wouldn't be writing this Introduction without the foresight of Calvin Lehew, Marilyn's husband.

Calvin recognized that my given name, Daisy, was the perfect embodiment of the warmth that we wanted the restaurant to reflect. Without knowing it, he helped launch my culinary career. Although Miss Daisy's closed in 1991, I have continued my love of cooking through my catering business, cookbook writing, public speaking, television and media appearances, culinary consulting, and being a spokesperson for Miss Daisy's line of foods (one of which is my Five Flavor Pound Cake, the recipe for which you'll find on page 34 of this book—look for it at your hometown supermarket).

I thank you, Calvin, for helping make Miss Daisy's a continued reality, and you, Marilyn, for helping make my Tearoom dream come true, and for your recipe contributions to this book.

Marilyn, Calvin, and I thank *you*, the patrons of Miss Daisy's Tearoom, the owners of *Recipes from Miss Daisy's*, and those of you who have enjoyed dining with these recipes throughout the years at our table or yours. May you and your families be richly blessed as you continue to serve these much-loved recipes.

Your thankful friend,
Daisy King
May 21, 2003

If you would like to get in touch with Miss Daisy, you can write to her in care of the publisher:

> *Cumberland House Publishing*
> *431 Harding Industrial Drive*
> *Nashville, Tennessee 37209*

or email her at missdaisyk@aol.com.

Luncheon at the Tearoom

The story of Daisy King's career in the restaurant business is as interesting as the food she serves. In the mid-1970s when Carter's Court in Franklin was still on the drawing board, the developers recognized the need for a place where ladies could go for lunch. After a turn-of-the-century house was moved back from Columbia Avenue to its present location, upon seeing it people exclaimed, "That's it. That's got to be a tearoom." Thus, the old house was given a new lease on life and with much work and ingenuity became Miss Daisy's Tearoom.

Persistence, determination, and *pride* were all words used to describe the opening of Miss Daisy's Tearoom. It was decided from the beginning that "only the best" quality foods would be served. No mass-produced, radar-range shortcuts would be taken. The menu would change several times a year, coordinating the food with the seasons. Daisy King personally greeted each customer, giving them the feeling of being both welcomed and honored. It was said that although you came to Miss Daisy's as a customer, you left as a friend.

The restaurant moved to Green Hills, a suburb of Nashville, in 1982, expanding to a full-service restaurant. During that decade Miss Daisy's had locations at Nashville shopping malls and in downtown Nashville.

National food and restaurant writers have paid tribute to Miss Daisy's, but, more important, so have the citizens of Tennessee. The original commitment to excellence became a Southern tradition, and guests have dined at Miss Daisy's from all over the United States.

```
┌─────────────────────────────────────────────┐
│  ┌───────────────────────────────────────┐  │
│  │           Turkey Divan                │  │
│  │        Frozen Cherry Salad            │  │
│  │           Bran Muffins                │  │
│  │          Buttermilk Pie               │  │
│  └───────────────────────────────────────┘  │
└─────────────────────────────────────────────┘
```

Turkey Divan

2	10-ounce packages frozen broccoli or 2 bunches fresh broccoli (do not overcook)
2	to 3 cups diced or sliced cooked turkey
Sauce	
2	10¾-ounce cans cream of chicken soup

½	cup shredded sharp Cheddar cheese
1	cup mayonnaise
1	teaspoon lemon juice
½	teaspoon curry powder
½	cup toasted breadcrumbs
1	tablespoon margarine

Preheat the oven to 350°. In a flat Pyrex dish place a layer of broccoli and turkey. In a large bowl mix the soup, Cheddar cheese, mayonnaise, lemon juice, and curry powder. Pour the sauce over the broccoli and turkey. Top with the breadcrumbs and margarine. Bake for 25 to 30 minutes. This can be made ahead of time and heated. Yield: 6 servings.

Frozen Cherry Salad

1	16-ounce can cherry pie filling
1	14-ounce can condensed milk
1	14-ounce can crushed pineapple

1	13-ounce carton whipped topping
	Party Salad Topping (see p. 59)
	Strawberries for garnish

In a large bowl mix all of the ingredients. Spread into a 9 x 13-inch pan and freeze. Cut into squares and garnish with Party Salad Topping and strawberries. Yield: 6 to 8 servings.

Bran Muffins

2 cups boiling water
6 cups bran cereal
1 heaping cup vegetable shortening
3 cups sugar
4 eggs

1 quart buttermilk
5 cups all-purpose flour
5 teaspoons baking soda
1 tablespoon salt
1 15-ounce box raisins (optional)

Preheat the oven to 400°. Grease the tins of a muffin pan. In a saucepan boil the water and add 2 cups bran cereal. Set aside. In a large bowl mix the shortening and sugar until soft. Add the eggs, and beat well. Add the buttermilk and scalded bran cereal. Into a medium bowl sift the flour, baking soda, and salt. Add the dry ingredients to the liquid mixture. You may have to transfer to a larger bowl when adding the dry ingredients. Stir in the remaining bran cereal and raisins, if desired. Bake in the prepared muffin tins for 15 to 20 minutes. This batter keeps in the refrigerator for a month, so bake only the muffins needed and refrigerate the remaining batter for future bakings. Yield: 36 muffins.

Buttermilk Pie

⅓ cup butter
1 cup sugar
3 egg yolks, beaten
3 tablespoons all-purpose flour
¼ teaspoon salt

1 teaspoon lemon juice
½ teaspoon grated lemon rind
1½ cups buttermilk
3 egg whites, stiffly beaten
1 unbaked 9-inch pie crust

Preheat the oven to 450°. In a large bowl mix the butter and sugar until soft. Add the egg yolks and beat well. Add the flour, salt, lemon juice, and lemon rind. Mix thoroughly. Add the buttermilk. Fold in the beaten egg whites. Pour the filling into the pie crust and bake for 10 minutes. Reduce the heat to 350° and bake for an additional 40 minutes. Yield: 6 servings.

```
┌─────────────────────────────────────────┐
│                                           │
│            Shrimp Creole                  │
│       Congealed Cucumber Salad            │
│          Sally Lunn Muffins               │
│            Heath Bar Cake                 │
│                                           │
└─────────────────────────────────────────┘
```

Shrimp Creole

¼ cup vegetable oil	1 tablespoon sugar
1 cup diced onion	1 tablespoon salt
1 cup diced celery	1 tablespoon chili powder
½ cup diced green pepper	2 pounds raw shrimp, cleaned
3½ cups canned tomatoes with juice	¼ cup all-purpose flour
1 8-ounce can tomato sauce	¼ cup water
2 bay leaves	⅛ teaspoon hot sauce

In a saucepan heat the oil and sauté the onion, celery, and pepper until tender. Add the tomatoes, tomato sauce, bay leaves, sugar, salt, and chili powder. Mix well. Simmer for 30 minutes. Remove the bay leaves. Add the shrimp. Simmer for an additional 30 minutes. In a medium bowl mix the flour and water to a paste. Add a cup or two of the tomato mixture and stir with a wire whisk until blended. Add the flour mixture to the tomato mixture. Add the hot sauce. Cook until the creole is thickened, about 5 minutes. Serve over rice. Yield: 6 to 8 servings.

Congealed Cucumber Salad

1 3-ounce package lemon gelatin	¾ teaspoon salt
½ cup hot water	1 tablespoon onion juice
1 8-ounce carton sour cream	2 tablespoons fresh lemon juice
½ cucumber, minced fine	

In a heatproof bowl dissolve the gelatin in the hot water and allow to cool completely. Beat in the sour cream. Add the remaining ingredients. Pour into a mold and congeal. Yield: 6 to 9 servings.

Sally Lunn Muffins

½ cup butter
½ cup sugar
3 cups all-purpose flour
4 teaspoons baking powder
1½ teaspoons salt

2 cups milk
½ cup light cream
½ cup heavy cream
3 eggs, beaten

Preheat the oven to 350°. Grease the tins of a muffin pan. In a large bowl mix the butter and sugar until light. In a medium bowl sift together the flour, baking powder, and salt. Add to the butter-sugar mixture, alternating with the milk and cream. Add the eggs. Mix well. Bake in the prepared muffin tins for 30 minutes. Yield: 24 small muffins.

Heath Bar Cake

1 cup packed dark brown sugar
½ cup sugar
½ cup butter
2 cups all-purpose flour

1 egg
1 cup buttermilk
1 teaspoon baking soda
7 regular-size Heath bars, broken into pieces

Preheat the oven to 350°. Grease and flour a 9 x 13-inch pan. In a medium bowl mix the brown sugar, sugar, butter, and flour as for a pie crust. Remove ½ cup and set aside. Add the egg, buttermilk, and baking soda to the rest of the mixture. Press into the bottom of the prepared pan. Sprinkle the remaining sugar-flour-butter mixture combined with broken Heath bars over the batter. Bake for 30 minutes. Yield: 6 to 8 servings.

Carter's Court Salad Bowl
Honey-French Dressing
Ice Cream Pecan Ball with Butterscotch Sauce

Carter's Court Salad Bowl

1	16-ounce carton cottage cheese	1	cup cooked French-style green beans
8	cups mixed salad greens		Black and green olives
2	tomatoes, cut into wedges		Cooked Asparagus spears
4	eggs, sieved		Paprika

To arrange individual salads: place a small dip of cottage cheese in the center of a clear glass plate or shallow bowl about 9 inches in diameter. Place the mixed greens around the cottage cheese. Garnish with the remaining ingredients, sprinkling a small amount of paprika on the cottage cheese. Yield: 6 to 8 servings.

Honey-French Dressing

1	cup vegetable oil	½	teaspoon dry mustard
¼	cup cider vinegar	½	teaspoon paprika
¼	cup lemon juice	⅓	cup honey
1	teaspoon salt		

In a medium bowl beat all of the ingredients together. Transfer to a jar or bottle. Store in the refrigerator. Shake well before serving.

Ice Cream Pecan Ball with Butterscotch Sauce

½ gallon vanilla ice cream
Chopped pecans
Butterscotch Sauce
1½ cups packed light brown
sugar

4 tablespoons butter
⅔ cup white corn syrup
⅔ cup evaporated milk

Form the ice cream into 8 large balls. Place the chopped pecans in a shallow dish, and roll the ice cream balls in them to coat. Freeze.

In a saucepan combine the sugar, butter, and corn syrup. Stir constantly over low heat until the sugar dissolves and the mixture boils. Stop stirring. Cook until the mixture forms a soft ball in cold water (240°). Cool slightly. Add the evaporated milk. Pour over the Ice Cream Pecan Balls. Yield: 8 servings.

Creamed Chicken

½ cup butter
½ cup all-purpose flour
1 teaspoon salt
2 cups chicken stock
2 cups light cream
2 cups milk
4 cups chopped cooked chicken

1 8-ounce can water chestnuts, sliced and drained
1 2-ounce jar pimientos, drained and chopped
¼ cup sherry (optional)

In a saucepan melt the butter. Add the flour and salt, and cook until bubbly. Add the chicken stock. Stir with a wire whisk until smooth. Add the cream and milk. Simmer for 30 minutes. Add the chicken, water chestnuts, pimientos, and sherry, and heat thoroughly when ready to serve. Yield: 8 servings.

Cornmeal Muffin Rings

1 cup self-rising cornmeal
1 tablespoon all-purpose flour (optional)
1 cup buttermilk

1 egg, slightly beaten
3 tablespoons bacon drippings or melted shortening
1 teaspoon sugar

Preheat the oven to 450°. Grease the muffin rings or pan. In a large bowl mix the dry ingredients. In a small bowl mix the buttermilk and egg and add to the dry ingredients. Pour in the bacon drippings or melted shortening and mix well. Bake in the prepared rings or pan for about 20 minutes. Yield: 6 to 8 servings.

Festive Cranberry Salad

1   3-ounce package orange gelatin
1   3-ounce package raspberry gelatin
2   cups boiling water

1   16-ounce can whole-berry cranberry sauce
1   14-ounce can crushed pineapple

In a heatproof bowl dissolve the gelatins in 2 cups boiling water. Add the cranberry sauce and crushed pineapple with juice. Mix well. Put in individual molds or a 9 x 9-inch dish. Congeal. Yield: 6 to 9 servings.

Marinated Carrots

2   pounds carrots
2   medium onions, diced
2   green peppers, chopped
1   10¾-ounce can tomato soup
¾   cup cider vinegar

½   cup corn oil
1   teaspoon Worcestershire sauce
1   teaspoon prepared mustard
¾   cup sugar

Peel and slice the carrots. Cook in salted water until tender. Drain. In a casserole dish arrange the carrots, onions, and peppers in layers. Make a marinade by combining the remaining ingredients. Pour the marinade over the carrots. Refrigerate for 24 hours before serving. The marinated carrots will keep in the refrigerator for over a week. Yield: 12 servings.

Fudge Pie

2   squares unsweetened chocolate
½   cup butter
2   eggs

1   cup sugar
2   tablespoons all-purpose flour
1   teaspoon vanilla extract
½   cup chopped walnuts

Grease a pie pan and set aside. Melt the chocolate and butter. Add the eggs, sugar, flour, vanilla, and nuts. Bake in the prepared pan at 325° for 30 minutes, starting in a cold oven. This pie is delicious served with peppermint ice cream. Yield: 6 servings.

Shrimp Aspic Mold with Horseradish Dressing
Toasted Cheese Muffins
Poppy Seed Cake

Shrimp Aspic Mold

1 6-ounce package lemon
   gelatin
1½ cups boiling water
½ cup chili sauce
2 cups tomato juice
1 tablespoon sweet pickle
   relish

½ cup chopped green olives
1 tablespoon minced onion
1 cup chopped celery
2 pounds cooked shrimp

In a heatproof bowl dissolve the gelatin in the boiling water.
Add the chili sauce and tomato juice. Chill until the mixture
begins to thicken. Add the remaining ingredients. Congeal.
Yield: 6 to 8 servings.

Horseradish Dressing

1 cup mayonnaise
2 tablespoons chili sauce

1 tablespoon prepared
   horseradish

In a medium bowl mix all of the ingredients together.
Transfer to a jar or bottle, and refrigerate.

Toasted Cheese Muffins

8 ounces Cheddar cheese, grated	1 teaspoon garlic salt
½ cup butter, softened	1 teaspoon onion salt
2 eggs, beaten	8 English muffins, cut into halves
½ cup chopped black olives	Paprika for garnish

Preheat the oven to 400°. In a large bowl blend the Cheddar cheese, butter, eggs, black olives, garlic salt, and onion salt using an electric mixer. Spread the mixture on the cut sides of the English muffin halves and place the muffins on a baking sheet. Sprinkle with paprika. Bake for 10 minutes. Yield: 16 servings.

Poppy Seed Cake

1 18.25-ounce package yellow cake mix	4 eggs
1 3.5-ounce package instant coconut pudding	½ cup poppy seeds
½ cup vegetable oil	2 cups prepared vanilla pudding
1 cup water	1 3.5-ounce package vanilla pie filling

Preheat the oven to 350°. Grease a tube pan. In a large bowl mix together the cake mix, coconut pudding, oil, water, eggs, poppy seeds, and vanilla pudding using an electric mixer. Bake in the prepared pan for 1 hour. When cool, cut the cake into three layers. Mix one package vanilla pie filling according to the package directions or make your own filling. Spread the pie filling between the layers and on top of the cake. Refrigerate the cake until serving time. Yield: 12 to 15 servings.

Garden Tomato Stuffed with Tearoom Tuna Salad
Hot French Cheese Sandwiches
Pecan Pie

Garden Tomato Stuffed with Tearoom Tuna Salad

3 7-ounce cans white tuna, drained
½ cup chopped celery
4 hard-boiled eggs, chopped
¼ cup sweet pickle relish
½ cup mayonnaise
8 medium-sized tomatoes
Note: White or Albacore tuna is a must for this salad.

Flake the tuna and place in a large bowl. Add the celery, eggs, pickle relish, and mayonnaise, and mix well. Chill. Prepare the tomatoes for stuffing. Stuff generously with the tuna mixture. Yield: 8 servings.

Hot French Cheese Sandwiches

½ pound sharp Cheddar cheese, grated
½ cup butter, softened
2 eggs
1 teaspoon garlic salt
1 teaspoon onion salt
16 slices white bread

Preheat the oven to 400°. In the bowl of a mixer blend the Cheddar cheese and butter. Add the eggs, garlic salt, and onion salt. Whip until creamy. Spread the mixture on one slice of bread, place another slice of bread on top, and spread it with the cheese mixture. Sprinkle with paprika. Cut into halves. Repeat with the remaining bread slices. Place the sandwiches on a baking sheet and bake for 10 to 15 minutes. These may be frozen and then baked as needed. Yield: 8 servings.

Pecan Pie

½ cup sugar
2 tablespoons butter
3 eggs, beaten
¼ teaspoon salt
1 teaspoon vanilla extract

1 cup light corn syrup
1 tablespoon all-purpose flour
1 cup pecans
1 unbaked 9-inch pie crust

Preheat the oven to 350°. In a large bowl mix the sugar and butter until soft. Add the eggs, salt, vanilla, corn syrup, flour, and pecans. Pour into the pie crust. Bake for 40 minutes. Yield: 6 servings.

```
┌─────────────────────────────────────────────┐
│  ┌───────────────────────────────────────┐  │
│  │           Tearoom Chili                │  │
│  │           Green Salad                  │  │
│  │           French Bread                 │  │
│  │        Sour Cream Pound Cake           │  │
│  └───────────────────────────────────────┘  │
└─────────────────────────────────────────────┘
```

Tearoom Chili

1 pound ground beef	1 16-ounce can chili beans or
1 medium onion, chopped	kidney beans
½ green pepper, diced	Water, if needed
1 package chili seasoning mix	
1 16-ounce can tomato sauce	
with bits	

In a saucepan sauté the beef, onion, and pepper. Add the remaining ingredients. Simmer for 2 hours before serving. Yield: 6 servings.

Sour Cream Pound Cake

1 cup butter, softened	½ teaspoon salt
2 cups sugar	¼ teaspoon baking soda
6 eggs	1 cup sour cream
3 cups sifted all-purpose flour	1 teaspoon vanilla extract

Preheat the oven to 350°. Grease a tube pan. In a large bowl mix the butter and sugar until light. Add the eggs one at a time, beating thoroughly after each addition. Sift the dry ingredients 3 times and add alternately with the sour cream to the first mixture, beating until smooth. Add the vanilla. Pour into the prepared pan. Bake for 1 hour and 20 minutes. Let stand in the pan on a cooling rack for about 5 minutes. This cake freezes well. Yield: 12 to 15 servings.

Corn and Ham Chowder

½ cup butter	1½ teaspoons salt
1 cup chopped celery	½ teaspoon pepper
½ cup chopped onion	½ teaspoon onion salt
2 cups diced cooked ham	½ teaspoon celery salt
3 10-ounce packages frozen cream-style corn	1 cup milk
	Fresh parsley for garnish

In a skillet melt the butter and sauté the celery, onion, and ham. Add the corn, salt, pepper, onion salt, celery salt, and milk. Heat. Simmer for 20 minutes before serving. Garnish with fresh parsley. Yield: 6 to 8 servings.

Hot Fruit Crisp

1 14 to 16-ounce can apple or peach pie filling	1 cup packed light brown sugar
½ cup butter, softened	½ teaspoon ground cinnamon
1 cup oatmeal	½ teaspoon grated nutmeg
1 cup all-purpose flour	

Preheat the oven to 350°. Pour the pie filling into a greased 9 x 9-inch baking dish. Slice the butter and dot the slices on top of the pie filling. In a large bowl mix together the oatmeal, flour, brown sugar, cinnamon, and nutmeg. Sprinkle this mixture over the pie filling and butter. Bake for 30 to 40 minutes. Yield: 6 to 9 servings.

Mexican Casserole

1 pound ground beef
1 medium onion, chopped
1 teaspoon salt
1 teaspoon pepper
1 8-ounce can tomato sauce
1 package chili seasoning mix
1 16-ounce can tomatoes with juice

1 16-ounce can chili beans or kidney beans, drained
½ pound sharp Cheddar cheese, grated
Corn chips

In a large skillet sauté the ground beef and onion. Add the salt and pepper. Add the tomato sauce, chili seasoning, and tomatoes. Cook over medium heat for 30 minutes.

Preheat the oven to 350°. Add the beans. Pour into a casserole and top with the cheese and corn chips. Bake for 20 minutes. Yield: 6 to 8 servings.

Flowerpot Dessert

8	sterile clay flowerpots, 2½ to 4-inch size	1	quart cherry vanilla ice cream
1	purchased small pound or angel food cake, crumbled into pieces		Whipped topping or whipped cream
			Shaved chocolate
½	cup dark rum or 2 ounces rum flavoring	8	5-inch straw pieces
		8	fresh flowers with some stem

Sprinkle half of the rum over the crumbled cake. Fill the flowerpots with 1 inch of the cake mixture. Mix the remaining half of the rum with the ice cream. Put the ice cream in the pots. Cover with whipped topping and sprinkle with shaved chocolate. Put a straw in the center of each pot so that 3 inches are showing. Put in the freezer until serving time. Put a fresh flower stem in each straw and serve. You can also use Miss Daisy's Five Flavor Pound Cake for this dessert (see p. 34). Yield: 8 servings.

Fresh Fruit Bowl with Poppy Seed Dressing
Finger Sandwiches
Lemon Supreme Cake

Fresh Fruit Bowl

Use any combination of the following fruits:

Peaches
Cherries
Grapes
Watermelon
Blueberries

Grapefruit
Honeydew melon
Cantaloupe
Strawberries
Pineapple
Bananas

Poppy Seed Dressing

¾ cup sugar
1   teaspoon salt
1   teaspoon dry mustard

1   cup vegetable oil
1½ tablespoons onion juice
2   tablespoons poppy seeds

In a small bowl mix the dry ingredients together. Add the vinegar. Mix well. Add the oil and beat until thick. Add the onion juice and poppy seeds. Transfer to a jar or bottle. Refrigerate until ready to use.

Pumpkin Bread for Finger Sandwiches

1 cup water
1 cup oil
1 21-ounce can pumpkin pie filling or 1 16-ounce can plain pumpkin
3 cups sugar
3 eggs
1 cup chopped black walnuts
1½ cups chopped dates

3½ cups self-rising flour
1 teaspoon nutmeg
1 teaspoon ground ginger
1 teaspoon salt
½ teaspoon ground cloves
½ teaspoon baking powder
2 teaspoons ground cinnamon
2 teaspoons baking soda

Preheat the oven to 325°. Grease 2 large loaf pans. In a large mixing bowl mix together the water, oil, pumpkin, sugar, eggs, walnuts, and dates. Into a separate bowl sift together the flour, nutmeg, ginger, salt, cloves, baking powder, cinnamon, and baking soda. Add to the pumpkin mixture, and mix well. Pour into the prepared pans. Bake for 1 hour and 30 minutes. Yield: 2 loaves.

Lemon Supreme Cake

1 18.25-ounce package lemon supreme cake mix
4 eggs
½ cup salad oil
1 3-ounce package lemon gelatin dissolved in 1 cup water

1 6-ounce can frozen lemonade concentrate
1 cup confectioners' sugar

Preheat the oven to 350°. In a large bowl mix the cake mix, eggs, oil, and gelatin. Grease and flour a square pan, 2-quart casserole, or tube pan. Pour the batter into the prepared pan and bake for 45 minutes. In a small bowl combine the lemonade concentrate and confectioners' sugar. Spread on top of the cake. Yield: 12 to 15 servings.

Miss Daisy's Beef Casserole
Green Salad
Hot French Bread
Fresh Carrot Cake with Cream Cheese Frosting

Miss Daisy's Beef Casserole

2	pounds lean ground beef	1	cup cubed American processed cheese
1	cup diced celery		
¼	cup diced green pepper	½	cup chopped green olives
¾	cup chopped onion	½	cup chopped black olives
1	29-ounce can tomatoes	½	teaspoon salt
1	16-ounce can tomatoes	¼	teaspoon pepper
1	8-ounce can mushroom pieces, drained	1	6-ounce package egg noodles, uncooked
1	8-ounce can water chestnuts, drained and sliced	2	cups shredded Cheddar cheese

Preheat the oven to 350°. In a large saucepan brown the beef. Pour off any accumulated grease. Add the celery, green pepper, and onion, and sauté. Add the tomatoes and their juice. Add the mushrooms, water chestnuts, American cheese, green olives, black olives, salt, pepper, and noodles. Simmer for 20 minutes. Pour into a 9 x 13-inch casserole dish. Spread the Cheddar cheese on top. Bake for 30 minutes. Yield: 12 to 15 servings.

Fresh Carrot Cake with Cream Cheese Frosting

4 eggs
1½ cups vegetable oil
2 cups all-purpose flour
2 cups sugar
2 teaspoons baking powder
2 teaspoons baking soda
3 teaspoons ground cinnamon
1 teaspoon salt
3 cups packed grated raw carrots
½ cup chopped black walnuts

Frosting
1 1-pound box confectioners' sugar
½ cup butter, softened
1 8-ounce package cream cheese
½ cup chopped black walnuts (optional)

Preheat the oven to 350°. Grease 3 9-inch layer pans. In a large bowl beat the eggs and oil. In a separate bowl mix the flour, sugar, baking powder, baking soda, cinnamon, and salt. Add to the egg and oil mixture. Beat well. Add the carrots and walnuts. Blend. Pour into the prepared pans. Bake for 25 minutes. Let cool before frosting.

In a large bowl blend the ingredients for the frosting. Spread the frosting on the cooled cake. Refrigerate the cake. Yield: 12 to 15 servings.

```
┌─────────────────────────────────────────────┐
│        Festive Shrimp Salad on Tomato Aspic  │
│            Crunchy Cheese Biscuits           │
│              Tangy Citrus Cake               │
└─────────────────────────────────────────────┘
```

Festive Shrimp Salad

1 pound cooked shrimp	1 tablespoon chopped green
1 cup chopped celery	onion
2 fresh tomatoes, peeled and	½ teaspoon salt
diced	⅛ teaspoon pepper
¼ cup chopped green pepper	Avocado wedges
2 tablespoons chopped	
pimientos	

In a large bowl combine the shrimp, celery, tomatoes, green
pepper, pimientos, green onion, salt, and pepper. Mix with
Sour Cream Dressing (see below). Serve on tomato aspic
squares and garnish with avocado wedges. Yield: 6 servings.

Sour Cream Dressing

1 cup sour cream	1 tablespoon lemon juice
½ cup catsup	2 teaspoons horseradish
1 tablespoon soy sauce	1 teaspoon salt
1 tablespoon grated onion	½ teaspoon dry mustard

In a large bowl blend all of the ingredients. Add to the
shrimp mixture.

Tomato Aspic

2 3-ounce packages lemon	2 cups tomato juice
gelatin	½ cup chili sauce
1½ cups boiling water	

In a heatproof bowl dissolve the gelatin in the boiling water.
Add the tomato juice and chili sauce. Pour into a 9 x 9-inch
pan. Congeal. Yield: 6 servings.

Recipes from Miss Daisy's

Crunchy Cheese Biscuits

½ cup butter
1 cup all-purpose flour
1 cup grated sharp Cheddar
cheese

½ teaspoon salt
1 cup crispy rice cereal

Preheat the oven to 350°. In a large bowl blend the butter and flour. Add the Cheddar cheese and salt. Mix well. Add the rice cereal. Form into balls and bake for about 10 minutes on an ungreased baking sheet. Yield: 12 servings.

Tangy Citrus Cake

2 medium oranges
1 18.25-ounce package lemon
cake mix

2 eggs
Sweetened whipped cream

Preheat the oven to 350°. Grease a tube or bundt pan. Grate, peel, and squeeze the juice from the oranges. Add enough water to the orange juice to measure 1⅓ cups. In a large bowl blend the cake mix (dry), eggs, orange peel, and juice mixture using an electric mixer on low speed for about 30 seconds. Beat on medium speed for 3 minutes, scraping the bowl frequently. Pour into the prepared pan and bake for 40 minutes. Serve with whipped cream. Yield: 12 servings.

Welsh Rabbit

Waldorf Salad

Chess Cake

Welsh Rabbit

1 pound sharp Cheddar
cheese
1½ cups heavy cream
2 teaspoons Worcestershire
sauce
½ teaspoon mustard
¼ teaspoon cayenne pepper

¼ teaspoon paprika
8 English muffins, halved and
toasted
16 slices fried bacon
16 tomato slices
Parsley flakes

In a double boiler melt the Cheddar cheese. Add the cream,
Worcestershire sauce, mustard, cayenne, and paprika. Heat.
To assemble: place 2 hot muffin halves on each plate, a
tomato on each muffin half, 2 strips of bacon, the cheese
sauce, and parsley flakes for garnish. Yield: 6 servings.

Waldorf Salad

8 cups chopped Red Delicious
apples
2 cups chopped celery
1 cup chopped English
walnuts

½ cup mayonnaise
½ cup sour cream

In a large salad bowl mix all of the ingredients together.
Refrigerate until ready to serve.

Chess Cake

1 cup butter	1 teaspoon baking powder
1 pound light brown sugar	1 cup chopped pecans
½ cup white sugar	1 teaspoon vanilla extract
4 eggs	Confectioners' sugar
2 cups sifted all-purpose flour	

Preheat the oven to 300°. Grease and flour a 9 x 13-inch pan. In a saucepan heat the butter and sugar over low heat. Add the eggs, flour, baking powder, pecans, and vanilla. Pour into the prepared pan. Bake for 40 to 50 minutes. Cool for 10 minutes. Cut into squares. Roll the squares in confectioners' sugar. This cake is good served with vanilla ice cream on the side. Yield: 6 to 9 servings.

```
┌─────────────────────────────────────────────────────────────┐
│                                                               │
│   Melange of Chipped Beef and Mushrooms over Chinese Noodles  │
│                    Congealed Beet Salad                       │
│                        Spoon Rolls                            │
│                    Five Flavor Pound Cake                     │
│                                                               │
└─────────────────────────────────────────────────────────────┘
```

Melange of Chipped Beef and Mushrooms over Chinese Noodles

2   10¾-ounce cans cream of mushroom soup

2   10¾-ounce cans chicken and rice soup

3   small packages chipped beef

1   8-ounce can mushroom pieces, drained

1   8-ounce can sliced water chestnuts, drained

3   3-ounce cans Chinese noodles

In a large saucepan combine the soup, chipped beef, mushroom pieces, and water chestnuts. Heat and serve over warmed Chinese noodles. Yield: 6 servings.

Congealed Beet Salad

1   6-ounce package lemon gelatin

2   cups hot water

¼   cup vinegar

½   teaspoon salt

2   tablespoons horseradish

2   tablespoons grated onion

1   16-ounce can diced beets with juice

1   cup grated cucumber (optional)

In a heatproof bowl dissolve the gelatin in the hot water. Add the vinegar, salt, horseradish, onion, beets, and cucumber. Congeal. Garnish with salad dressing. Yield: 6 to 9 servings.

Spoon Rolls

1   package dry yeast
2   tablespoons warm water
     (110°)
2   cups warm water

¾   cup vegetable oil
4   cups self-rising flour
¼   cup sugar
1   egg

Preheat the oven to 400°. Grease the tins of a muffin pan. Dissolve the yeast in 2 tablespoons water. In a large bowl combine the dissolved yeast with the warm water, vegetable oil, flour, sugar, and egg. Spoon into the prepared muffin tins. Bake for 15 to 20 minutes. The batter will keep in the refrigerator for several days, so it may be made ahead of time and baked when needed. Yield: 24 to 30 small rolls.

Miss Daisy's Five Flavor Pound Cake

1 cup butter or margarine	1 cup milk
½ cup vegetable shortening	1 teaspoon coconut extract
3 cups sugar	1 teaspoon rum extract
5 eggs, well beaten	1 teaspoon butter extract
3 cups all-purpose flour	1 teaspoon lemon extract
½ teaspoon baking powder	1 teaspoon vanilla extract

Preheat the oven to 325°. Grease a 10-inch tube pan. In a large bowl mix the butter, shortening, and sugar until light and fluffy. In a small bowl beat the eggs until lemon colored. Add to the butter mixture. In a large bowl combine the flour and baking powder. Add to the butter mixture alternately with the milk. Stir in the flavorings. Spoon the mixture into the prepared pan and bake for 1 hour and 30 minutes, or until the cake tests done. Add glaze if desired (see below) or cool in the pan for about 10 minutes before turning out. This cake has become my signature recipe. Yield: 15 to 20 servings.

Glaze

1 cup sugar	1 teaspoon lemon extract
½ cup water	1 teaspoon rum extract
1 teaspoon coconut extract	1 teaspoon vanilla extract
1 teaspoon butter extract	

In a saucepan combine all of the ingredients and bring to a boil. Pour over the hot cake in the pan. Let the cake sit in the pan until cool.

```
┌─────────────────────────────────────────────────┐
│                                                   │
│   Hot Tuna Sandwich with Mushroom Cheese Sauce    │
│                  Corn Relish                      │
│                  Lemon Freeze                     │
│                                                   │
└─────────────────────────────────────────────────┘
```

Hot Tuna Sandwich

2 7-ounce cans white tuna,
   drained
1 10¾-ounce can cream of
   mushroom soup
6 hard-boiled eggs, chopped
¼ cup salad dressing

½ teaspoon salt
1 teaspoon minced onion
¼ cup chopped pimientos
½ cup chopped green pepper
16 slices bread

Preheat the oven to 350°. In a large bowl mix together the
tuna, soup, eggs, salad dressing, salt, onion, pimientos, and
green pepper. Spread this mixture between slices of bread,
making 8 sandwiches. Butter the top and bottom of each
sandwich. Place in a shallow pan. Bake for 25 minutes. Serve
with Mushroom Cheese Sauce (see below). Yield: 8 servings.

Mushroom Cheese Sauce

½ cup butter
½ cup all-purpose flour
½ teaspoon salt
⅛ teaspoon pepper
4 cups milk
2 8-ounce cans mushroom
   pieces

1 10¾-ounce can cream of
   mushroom soup
½ pound Cheddar cheese,
   grated

Make a white sauce: in a saucepan heat the butter. Add the
flour, salt, and pepper. When bubbly, add the milk slowly, stirring constantly. Bring to a boil. Add the mushroom pieces,
soup, and Cheddar cheese. Heat until the cheese melts.

Corn Relish

4	cups frozen yellow corn	1	green pepper, chopped
1½	cups grated cabbage	1	onion, chopped
½	cup diced celery	½	cup sugar
1	2-ounce jar pimientos, chopped	1	tablespoon dry mustard
		1½	cups vinegar
1	teaspoon salt		

In a saucepan mix together all of the ingredients. Bring to a boil and simmer for 20 minutes. Cool. Refrigerate for 24 hours before serving.

Lemon Freeze

	Graham cracker crumbs	¼	cup lemon juice
1	15-ounce can evaporated milk, chilled	¼	teaspoon lemon extract
		2	drops yellow food coloring
1	cup sugar		

Line a 9 x 9-inch pan with graham cracker crumbs. In a medium bowl whip the well-chilled evaporated milk until thick. Add the sugar, lemon juice, lemon extract, and yellow food coloring. Pour into the pan over the graham cracker crumbs. Freeze. Cut into squares to serve. Garnish as desired. Yield: 6 to 8 servings.

Quiche Lorraine

4	tablespoons butter	2	egg yolks
4	small onions, minced	2	eggs
1	teaspoon salt	1½	cups light cream
1	teaspoon pepper	⅛	teaspoon grated nutmeg
6	slices bacon, fried and crumbled	1	teaspoon chopped chives
1	cup shredded Gruyère or Swiss cheese	1	unbaked 9-inch pie crust

Preheat the oven to 350°. In a saucepan melt the butter and sauté the onions until soft. Season with the salt and pepper. Drain the onions and put in the bottom of the pie crust. Add the bacon. Sprinkle with the cheese. In a medium bowl beat together the egg yolks, eggs, light cream, nutmeg, and chives. Pour into the pie crust. Bake for 30 minutes. Let set about 5 minutes before cutting. Yield: 4 to 6 servings.

Apricot Nectar Cake

1   18.25-ounce package yellow
    or lemon cake mix
1   3-ounce box lemon gelatin

1   cup vegetable oil
1   cup apricot nectar
6   eggs

Preheat the oven to 350°. In a large bowl mix the ingredients together using an electric mixer, and bake in an ungreased 10-inch tube pan for 50 minutes or until done. Yield: 12 to 15 servings.

Glaze for Apricot Nectar Cake

2   cups confectioners' sugar
1   lemon, juiced and rind
    grated

1   cup orange juice

In a small bowl mix together the confectioners' sugar, lemon juice, lemon rind, and orange juice, and pour over the cooled cake while in the pan.

```
┌─────────────────────────────────────────┐
│  ┌───────────────────────────────────┐   │
│  │  Grandmother Hubbard's Frozen Fruit Salad │   │
│  │         Tea Punch                 │   │
│  │       Finger Sandwiches           │   │
│  │         Chess Pie                 │   │
│  └───────────────────────────────────┘   │
└─────────────────────────────────────────┘
```

Grandmother Hubbard's Frozen Fruit Salad

1   16-ounce can apricots, chopped
1   16-ounce can pears, chopped
1   small bottle red cherry halves
1   16-ounce can crushed pineapple
1   11-ounce can mandarin orange slices
2   bananas, sliced
1   cup chopped pecans (optional)

Dressing
2   eggs, beaten
4   tablespoons vinegar
4   tablespoons sugar
1   small jar marshmallow cream
1   6-ounce carton whipped topping
    Party Salad Topping (see p. 59)
    Fresh strawberries

Drain the fruits and combine in a large bowl. Set aside.
In a heavy pan combine the eggs, vinegar, and sugar. Cook
until thick, stirring constantly. Remove from heat. Cool. Add
the marshmallow cream and whipped topping. Add to the
fruit and mix well. Pour into individual molds. Freeze for 24
hours. Garnish with Party Salad Topping and fresh strawberries. Yield: 12 servings.

Tea Punch

7 tea bags	2 6-ounce cans frozen
2 cups sugar	lemonade concentrate
2 6-ounce cans frozen orange	Water to make 1 gallon
juice concentrate	Sprigs of fresh mint

Brew the tea. In a large punch bowl mix the sugar, orange juice concentrate, lemonade concentrate, and water. (You may add other juices such as peach, pear, pineapple, apricot. Remember to cut down on the amount of sugar when you add these sweetened juices.) Add the tea. Garnish with sprigs of fresh mint. Yield: 1 gallon. (If extra juices are added, you will have more than 1 gallon.)

Miss Daisy's Pimiento Cheese Sandwich Filling

1 4-ounce can pimientos, drained and chopped	1 clove garlic, minced
½ cup mayonnaise	⅓ cup finely chopped fresh parsley
¼ cup Durkee's sauce	¼ teaspoon sugar
2 tablespoons Dijon mustard	1 pound (16 ounces) sharp Cheddar cheese, grated
⅛ teaspoon cayenne pepper	

In a large bowl combine all of the ingredients except the Cheddar cheese and mix well. Add the cheese and mix again. Refrigerate. To serve, spread on fresh white bread. Crust is optional. Yield: 3½ cups.

Chess Pie

½ cup butter, melted	1 teaspoon all-purpose flour
1 tablespoon vinegar	1 teaspoon cornmeal
3 eggs, well beaten	1½ cups sugar
1 teaspoon vanilla extract	1 unbaked 9-inch pie crust

Preheat the oven to 300°. In a large bowl combine the ingredients. Pour into the pie crust. Bake until brown. Reduce the heat to 200° and continue baking for 40 minutes. Yield: 6 servings.

```
┌─────────────────────────────────────────────┐
│              Ham and Yeast Rolls              │
│                Cheese Soufflé                 │
│               Pink Arctic Freeze              │
│                  Dump Cake                    │
└─────────────────────────────────────────────┘
```

Cheese Soufflé

7   slices bread, crusts removed
2½ cups milk
1   teaspoon salt
⅛   teaspoon garlic powder
⅛   teaspoon cayenne pepper

1   teaspoon Worcestershire sauce
8   ounces sharp Cheddar cheese, grated
3   eggs, separated

Butter a 2-quart casserole dish. In a large bowl soak the bread slices in the milk, and break them into tiny bits. Add the salt, garlic powder, cayenne, Worcestershire sauce, and cheese. Beat the egg yolks and whites separately; fold both into the bread-cheese mixture. Put in the prepared casserole dish. Start in a cold oven and bake at 350° for 1 hour. Yield: 6 servings.

Pink Arctic Freeze

1   8-ounce package cream cheese, softened
2   tablespoons mayonnaise
2   tablespoons sugar
1   16-ounce can whole-berry cranberry sauce

1   cup crushed pineapple, drained
1   cup heavy cream, whipped

In a large bowl beat the cream cheese, mayonnaise, and sugar using an electric mixer. Add the cranberry sauce and pineapple. Mix well. Fold in the whipped cream. Freeze in a 9 x 9-inch dish. Cut into squares to serve. Yield: 6 to 8 servings.

Dump Cake

1 20-ounce can crushed
   pineapple
1 3½-ounce can flaked
   coconut
1 cup packed dark brown
   sugar

1 18.25-ounce package yellow
   cake mix
1 cup butter
1 cup chopped nuts

Preheat the oven to 300°. Oil a 9 x 13-inch pan. Dump the
can of pineapple with juice into the pan and spread over the
bottom. Sprinkle the coconut, then the brown sugar, then the
yellow cake mix, and spread evenly. Cut the butter into thin
slices and dot over the cake. Sprinkle the nuts over top. Bake
for 1 hour. Cut into squares and serve with vanilla ice cream.
Yield: 12 to 16 servings.

Split Pea Soup with Sherry

¼ cup butter	2 10½-ounce cans split pea soup
¼ cup chopped onion	1½ soup cans milk
¼ cup chopped celery	¼ cup sherry
¼ cup chopped carrots	Fresh snipped parsley for
2 cups chopped cooked ham	garnish

In a saucepan heat the butter and sauté the onion, celery, and carrot. Add the ham. Simmer for 10 minutes. Add the soup, milk, and sherry. Heat and serve. Garnish with fresh snipped parsley. Yield: 6 to 8 servings.

Pumpkin Squares

4 eggs	⅛ teaspoon salt
2 cups sugar	2 teaspoons baking soda
1 cup vegetable oil	2 teaspoons ground cinnamon
2 cups all-purpose flour	2 cups pumpkin pie filling

Preheat the oven to 350°. Grease a 12 x 18-inch pan. In a large bowl mix together the eggs, sugar, and oil. Into a separate bowl sift together the flour, salt, baking soda, and cinnamon. Add to the egg mixture. Blend in the pumpkin pie filling. Pour into the prepared pan. Bake for 25 to 30 minutes. Cut into squares to serve. Yield: 12 to 15 servings.

Cream Cheese Frosting

½ cup butter, softened	1 teaspoon vanilla extract
1 1-pound box confectioners' sugar	1 cup chopped walnuts
1 8-ounce package cream cheese, softened	

In a large bowl mix the ingredients together and spread over the cooled pumpkin cake.

Miss Daisy at Home

The reasons for Daisy's success differ according to the teller, but there is no question that each one begins and ends with the lady herself. Her earliest memories of food date back to her grandparents' farm in Georgia, where she learned first about "Southern Style" food from the garden to the table. After graduation from Belmont College, Daisy taught home economics at colleges and high schools in Nashville; did free-lance work for a national grocery chain as a home economist; and, finally, her catering with a friend led to her meeting Calvin and Marilyn Lehew. A partnership ensued, and Miss Daisy's Restaurant became a reality.

At home, Daisy moved easily into the role of mother to two active boys and wife to Wayne King, who passed away in 1998. The Kings enjoyed entertaining in their home as well as dining out. And, like most good cooks, Daisy often tried new recipes on her own family over the years, always looking for new and interesting ways to prepare and serve food.

Outside of work, Daisy enjoys working in her yard, doing needlepoint, and reading cookbooks. However, first and fore-most, Daisy's hobby is people. Her bubbly personality and her astounding memory for names and faces indicate how very much Daisy enjoys meeting people. She believes every friend-ship is a special treasure.

Early in life Daisy was taught that every day is important. Her philosophy is simply to do your best each day and enjoy whatever the day brings. At home or at work, Daisy King is truly a remarkable lady.

Appetizers

Hot Broccoli Dip

½ cup butter
1 onion, chopped
1 10¾-ounce can mushroom soup
1 4-ounce can chopped mushrooms

1 roll garlic cheese
1 10-ounce package frozen chopped broccoli, cooked

In a saucepan heat the butter and sauté the onions until clear. Add the soup, mushrooms (with liquid), and garlic cheese until it melts. Add the cooked broccoli. Serve hot with your favorite crackers. Yield: 6 to 8 servings.

Chili Con Queso

1 pound processed cheese
1 large can tomatoes, drained

1 can hot green chiles
Onion juice

In a double boiler melt the cheese. Add the tomatoes and green chiles. Add a little onion juice to taste. Serve with corn chips or crackers. Yield: 2 to 3 cups.

Crab Dip Divine

1 12 to 14-ounce bottle catsup
1 12 to 14-ounce bottle chili sauce
¼ cup horseradish
Juice of 1 lemon

⅛ teaspoon hot sauce
⅛ teaspoon Worcestershire sauce
2 6½-ounce cans flaked crabmeat

Blend all ingredients together. Chill. Serve in a pineapple shell with crisp crackers. Yield: 3 cups.

Curry Dip

1	pint salad dressing	5	tablespoons catsup
1	garlic clove, crushed	5	tablespoons curry powder
3	tablespoons grated onion	1	tablespoon salt
1½	tablespoons Worcestershire sauce	1	teaspoon hot sauce

In a medium bowl combine all of the ingredients. Mix well. Refrigerate before serving. Yield: 3 cups.

Guacamole Dip

4	ripe avocados	2	teaspoons lemon juice
2	teaspoons onion juice		Salt
2	ripe tomatoes, diced and drained		Cayenne pepper
			French dressing

Sieve the avocado. Add the onion juice, tomatoes, lemon juice, salt, and cayenne pepper. Add French dressing until the desired consistency is obtained. Yield: 2 cups.

Shrimp Dip

1	8-ounce package cream cheese	½	teaspoon salt
2	cups finely chopped boiled shrimp	½	teaspoon Worcestershire sauce
1	cup sour cream	2	teaspoons lemon juice
		½	teaspoon hot sauce

In a large bowl combine all of the ingredients. Blend well. Refrigerate for several hours before serving. Yield: 4 cups.

Sour Cream and Onion Dip

1   pint sour cream   1   envelope onion soup mix

In a small bowl combine the sour cream and soup mix. Serve
with potato chips. Yield: 2½ cups.

Black-Eyed Susans

¼   pound sharp cheese, grated   Dates
1   cup butter   Pecan halves
½   teaspoon salt
3   cups sifted all-purpose flour

Preheat the oven to 450°. In a large bowl mix the cheese and
butter until soft. In a separate bowl combine the salt and the
flour. Add to the cheese mixture. Place 1 teaspoon mix on an
ungreased baking sheet; flatten. In the middle of the flat-
tened mix add a date and wrap the mix around the date.
Place a pecan half on top. Bake for 10 to 15 minutes. Yield: 6
dozen.

Cheese Ball

1   pound Cheddar cheese,   Worcestershire and hot
    grated   sauce, if desired
1   pound cream cheese   Chopped parsley or walnuts
1   onion, grated

In a large bowl mix the Cheddar cheese, cream cheese,
onion, and sauces, if desired. Form into a ball. Roll in
chopped parsley or walnuts. Yield: 12 servings.

Cheese Straws

¼ pound Cheddar cheese, grated
1 cup all-purpose flour

½ cup butter
⅛ teaspoon salt
⅛ teaspoon paprika

Preheat the oven to 350°. In a large bowl mix all of the ingredients together thoroughly. Roll or cut into straw shapes and place on a baking sheet. Bake for 12 minutes. Yield: 3 dozen.

Cucumber Ball

1 8-ounce package cream cheese
1 large cucumber, chopped
2 teaspoons mayonnaise

½ small onion, grated
⅛ teaspoon hot sauce
⅛ teaspoon Worcestershire sauce

In a large bowl mix all of the ingredients. Form the mixture into a ball, wrap in foil, and refrigerate. Yield: 8 to 10 servings.

Poppy Seed Squares

1 pound Cheddar cheese, grated
1 cup butter, softened

Poppy seeds
5 dozen toast squares

Preheat the oven to 350°. In a large bowl mix the Cheddar cheese and butter well. Spread on the toast squares and place on a baking sheet. Sprinkle with the poppy seeds and heat until toasted. Yield: 5 dozen.

Marinated Mushrooms

120 fresh button mushrooms	2½ cups olive oil
20 lemons (for 5 cups juice)	Salt and pepper

Wash and peel the mushrooms. Place groups of 24 mushrooms in shallow dishes and pour the juice of 4 lemons and ½ cup olive oil over each group. Marinate for at least 2 hours. Drain and serve with individual colored cocktail picks. Yield: 120 mushrooms.

Stuffed Mushrooms

36 fresh button mushrooms	2 tablespoons dry breadcrumbs
1 tablespoon oil	
1 tablespoon butter	Salt and pepper to taste
1 tablespoon minced onion	Milk

Wash and wipe the mushrooms carefully. Remove the centers and stems. In a heavy skillet heat the oil and butter. Place the mushrooms in the skillet, hollow side up, and season with salt and pepper. Cook over medium heat for 10 minutes. Drain on paper towels. In the same pan sauté the onion, chopped stems, and centers for about 5 minutes. Add the dry breadcrumbs, salt, and pepper, and just enough milk to moisten. Fill the mushroom caps with the stuffing. Keep covered and refrigerated until ready to serve. Just before serving, heat for 15 minutes in a 350° oven. Yield: 3 dozen.

Recipes from Miss Daisy's

Toasted Mushroom Rolls

2 pounds fresh mushrooms,
   diced
1 cup butter
¾ cup all-purpose flour
1 teaspoon salt

4 cups light cream
2½ tablespoons minced chives
4 teaspoons lemon juice
4 sandwich loaves of white
   bread, crusts trimmed

Preheat the oven to 400°. Peel the mushrooms and dice. In a saucepan heat the butter and sauté the mushrooms for 5 minutes. Blend in the flour and salt. Stir in the light cream and simmer until thick. Add the minced chives and lemon juice. Blend well. Remove the crusts from the bread and roll the slices thin. Spread with the mixture and roll up. Cut in half and toast on all sides for about 20 minutes in the oven. These are true delicacies and can be made far in advance to freeze for future use. If you plan to freeze them, don't toast until ready to serve. Yield: 13 dozen.

Nuts and Bolts

¾ cup butter, melted
4 teaspoons garlic salt
4 teaspoons celery salt
4 teaspoons Worcestershire
   sauce
2 teaspoons hot sauce

1 16-ounce can mixed nuts
1 box Corn Chex
1 box Wheat Chex
1 box Rice Chex
1 box Cheese Nips
1 box pretzels

Preheat the oven to 200°. In a small bowl blend together the melted butter, garlic salt, celery salt, Worcestershire sauce, and hot sauce. Combine the dry ingredients in a pan and add the butter mixture. Mix well and bake for 2 hours, stirring every 15 minutes. Yield:

Peppery Spiced Nuts

2   tablespoons butter, melted
1   pound pecan or walnut
    halves
2   teaspoons Worcestershire
    sauce

⅛   teaspoon hot sauce
½   teaspoon salt
¼   teaspoon pepper

Preheat the oven to 325°. In a skillet heat the butter and
sauté the pecan or walnut halves until hot. Add the remaining ingredients. Arrange the nuts in a shallow pan and bake
for 20 minutes. Yield: 4 cups.

Smoked Turkey Fingers

100 thin slices smoked turkey
1   8-ounce package cream
    cheese

Paprika for garnish

Spread thin slices of smoked turkey with cream cheese. Roll
up each slice. Sprinkle with paprika and serve. Yield: 100 fingers. (Ham or corned beef may also be used for this recipe.)

Beverages

Hot Spiced Apple Cider

9 46-ounce cans apple juice
2 teaspoons ground cinnamon
2 teaspoons grated nutmeg
2 teaspoons ground allspice
2 teaspoons ground cloves

In a large saucepan or stockpot blend all ingredients together and heat thoroughly. Yield: 100 4-ounce servings.

Hot Chocolate Mix

1 2-pound box instant chocolate drink mix
1 1-pound box confectioners' sugar
1 11-ounce jar powdered creamer
1 8-quart box powdered milk

In a large bowl mix the ingredients together and sift. Store in jars. To serve, fill a cup half full of mix and finish filling with hot water. Makes a nice gift.

Coca-Cola Punch

Juice of 12 lemons
3 cups sugar
5 pints water
6 20-ounce bottles of Coca Cola

In a punch bowl combine the lemon juice, sugar, and water. Let stand overnight in the refrigerator. When ready to serve add the Coca-Colas and ice. This is a good punch for children. Yield: 25 punch cup servings.

Cran-Orange Punch

1 gallon cranberry juice   1 gallon orange juice

In a punch bowl mix the juices and serve over ice cubes. A sprig of fresh mint completes this beverage. Yield: 2 gallons.

Hot Cranberry Tea

1 quart cranberry juice	Juice of 2 oranges
½ cup (scant) candy red hots	Juice of 2 lemons
2 cups sugar	Red food coloring
2 cups water	

In a large saucepan combine the cranberry juice and red hots. Heat slowly and stir until the red hots dissolve. Add the sugar and water and heat until the sugar dissolves. Add the orange and lemon juices. Dilute with water to suit taste. Add the red food coloring to desired color. Yield: 15 servings.

Hot Spiced Tea

2 cups orange-flavored instant breakfast drink	½ cup instant tea
1 cup sugar	1 teaspoon ground cinnamon
1 10-ounce package dry lemonade mix	1 teaspoon ground cloves

Mix the ingredients. Keep covered in a glass jar. Use 1 to 2 teaspoons per cup of water. Yield: 32 cups.

Sangria

½ pound strawberries, washed and halved

2 ripe peaches, peeled and cut into small pieces

1 orange, thinly sliced

1 lime, thinly sliced

Juice and rind of 1 lemon

½ cup sugar

¾ teaspoon ground cinnamon

2 bottles red wine

In a pitcher mix all of the ingredients, add the wine, and stir thoroughly, mashing the fruit slightly. Let stand at room temperature for at least 1 hour. Just before serving, add 20 ice cubes and stir until cold. Yield: 8 servings.

Hot V-8

V-8 juice
Beef bouillon
Celery salt

Hot sauce
Worcestershire sauce

Use equal parts of V-8 juice and beef bouillon. Add celery salt, hot sauce, and Worcestershire sauce to taste, and heat thoroughly.

Salads

Apricot Salad

1 20-ounce can crushed pineapple	1 pint sour cream
2 16-ounce cans apricots	1 envelope plain gelatin (optional, for extra thickening if needed)
1 6-ounce package apricot gelatin	

In a saucepan heat the juice from the cans of pineapple and apricots. Add the apricot gelatin and stir to dissolve. In a large bowl mix the apricots, pineapple, and sour cream. Add to the cooled gelatin. Mix and pour into molds. Yield: 24 servings.

Bing Cherry Salad

2 3-ounce packages black cherry gelatin	1 16-ounce can Bing cherries, drained
3 cups boiling water	1 cup finely chopped celery
Juice drained from cherries plus water to make 1 cup liquid	2 tablespoons lemon juice
	1 cup finely chopped pecans

In a saucepan dissolve the gelatin in the boiling water. Add the cherry juice–water mixture. Add the remaining ingredients. Chill until firm. The salad may be frozen if desired. Yield: 12 servings.

Congealed Green Pea Salad

1	3-ounce package lemon gelatin	1	cup small green peas, drained
1¾	cups hot water	1	cup chopped celery
½	cup nuts	1	cup sliced green olives

In a large bowl dissolve the gelatin in the hot water. Cool. When it begins to thicken, add the other ingredients and mold. Serve with mayonnaise on lettuce. Yield: 6 servings.

Black-Eyed Pea Salad—Greek-Style

4	15-ounce cans black-eyed peas, drained	½	teaspoon oregano leaves crushed between palms
1	cup diced celery	¼	cup plus 2 tablespoons vegetable oil
1	cup chopped scallions (include 2 to 3 inches of green ends)	¼	cup plus 2 tablespoons vinegar
¼	teaspoon (scant) garlic powder		

In a large bowl mix all ingredients well. Marinate, stirring occasionally, overnight. Yield: 10 to 12 servings.

Pineapple Salad Supreme

2	tablespoons plain gelatin	½	cup chopped pimientos
½	cup cold water	1	tablespoon sugar
1	20-ounce can crushed pineapple	¾	cup salad dressing
1	pint cottage cheese	½	pint heavy cream, whipped
1	green pepper, chopped	1	cup nuts

In the top of a double boiler dissolve the gelatin in the cold water. Heat over hot water to liquid consistency. In a large bowl combine the remaining ingredients. Add the dissolved gelatin. Congeal. Yield: 12 servings.

Peppermint Stick Candy Salad

1   3-ounce package lime gelatin
1   cup hot water
¾   cup pineapple juice
½   pint heavy cream, whipped
1   14-ounce can crushed
    pineapple
¾   cup chopped pecans
6   sticks peppermint candy,
    crushed

In a heatproof bowl dissolve the gelatin in the hot water. Add the pineapple juice. Chill until firm, then beat until fluffy. Next, fold in the whipped cream. Complete by adding the pineapple, nuts, and half of the crushed candy sticks. Chill until ready to serve. Sprinkle the remaining crushed candy on top of the salad. Yield: 8 to 10 servings.

Seven-Cup Salad

1   cup grated coconut
1   cup cottage cheese
1   cup sour cream
1   cup chopped nuts
1   cup crushed pineapple
1   cup fruit cocktail
1   cup miniature marshmallows

In a large bowl combine all of the ingredients and refrigerate. This salad improves after it sets a day or two. Yield: 6 servings.

Orange Sherbet Salad

1   6-ounce package orange
    gelatin
2   cups boiling water
1   pint orange sherbet
1   11-ounce can mandarin
    orange slices
2   bananas, sliced
1   8-ounce can crushed
    pineapple

In a heatproof bowl dissolve the gelatin in the boiling water. Add the sherbet, and stir until dissolved. Add the remaining ingredients. Refrigerate until congealed. Yield: 6 servings.

Recipes from Miss Daisy's

Summer Salad

1 3-ounce package lime gelatin	½ pint heavy cream
1 cup hot water	1 8-ounce can crushed
2 cups miniature marshmallows	pineapple
	½ cup chopped pecans
1 3-ounce package cream cheese	

In a large bowl dissolve the gelatin in the hot water; when it begins to thicken, add the marshmallows and other ingredients. Whip the cream before adding to the mixture. Chill. Serve on lettuce. Yield: 6 servings.

Party Salad Topping

1 4½-ounce carton whipped topping	¼ cup instant breakfast orange drink mix
¼ cup salad dressing	

In a small bowl combine the whipped topping, salad dressing, and drink mix. Mix well. Refrigerate until serving time.

Vegetables

Best Baked Beans

2   green peppers, finely chopped
1   small onion, finely chopped
½   cup brown sugar
½   cup catsup
1   teaspoon mustard
1   teaspoon Worcestershire sauce
1   20 to 24-ounce can pork and beans
6   slices bacon

Preheat the oven to 325°. In a casserole dish combine all of the ingredients, arranging the bacon across the top. Bake uncovered for 1 hour and 30 minutes to 2 hours. Yield: 6 servings.

Green Bean Casserole

1   16-ounce can French-style green beans or 1 package frozen green beans, cooked
½   onion, chopped
5   to 6 stalks celery, chopped
1   10¾-ounce can cream of chicken soup
1   6-ounce can bean sprouts
1   6-ounce can water chestnuts, sliced thin
    Grated cheese to cover top of casserole
1   2.8-ounce can French-fried onion rings

Preheat the oven to 350°. In a casserole dish layer the vegetables, soup, and water chestnuts. Sprinkle the cheese and onion rings over the top. Bake for 30 minutes. Yield: 6 servings.

Broccoli with Horseradish Dressing

½ cup water
¼ teaspoon salt
1 10-ounce package frozen broccoli

½ cup salad dressing
1 teaspoon sugar
2 tablespoons horseradish mustard

In a saucepan bring the water and salt to a boil. Add the frozen broccoli. When the second boil has been reached, reduce the heat to low and cook for 5 to 8 minutes. In a small bowl blend together the salad dressing, sugar, and horseradish mustard. Put a generous helping of dressing on each serving of broccoli. Yield: 6 servings.

Baked Limas with Sour Cream

1 pound dried lima beans
3 teaspoons salt
½ cup margarine
¾ cup brown sugar

1 tablespoon dry mustard
1 tablespoon molasses
1 cup sour cream

Soak the beans overnight in water. The next morning drain the beans and cover them with fresh water. Preheat the oven to 350°. Add 1 teaspoon salt and cook until tender, about 30 to 45 minutes. Drain again and rinse under hot water. Transfer to a casserole and dot margarine over the beans. In a small bowl mix the brown sugar, dry mustard, and the remaining salt and sprinkle over the beans. Stir in the molasses and finally pour the sour cream over the bean mixture and mix tenderly. Bake for 1 hour. Yield: 6 servings.

Eggplant Soufflé

2 cups diced peeled eggplant	1 cup grated cheese
1 cup breadcrumbs	3 eggs, beaten
1 cup milk	1 teaspoon black pepper
1½ teaspoons onion	1 teaspoon salt
2 tablespoons butter	

In a saucepan soak the eggplant in salt water for 1 hour. Preheat the oven to 350°. Butter a casserole dish. Drain the eggplant well, and cook until done. Mash the eggplant and add the remaining ingredients. Pour into the prepared casserole and bake for 30 to 45 minutes. Yield: 6 servings.

Onion Casserole

4 cups sliced onion, cooked in salted water until tender and drained	⅓ cup melted butter
	1 cup cornflake crumbs
	½ cup slivered almonds
1 10¾-ounce can cream of mushroom soup	

Preheat the oven to 350° to 375°. In a casserole dish mix all of the ingredients together, topping with the almonds. Bake until bubbly hot. Yield: 6 servings.

Party Squash

1 pound yellow squash, sliced	½ cup chopped pecans
1 teaspoon sugar	1 egg, slightly beaten
½ cup mayonnaise	½ cup grated Cheddar cheese
½ cup minced onion	Salt and pepper to taste
¼ cup finely chopped green pepper	Bread or cracker crumbs
	¼ cup butter

Preheat the oven to 350°. In a large saucepan cook the squash, drain, and mash. Add the sugar, mayonnaise, onion, green pepper, pecans, egg, Cheddar cheese, salt, and pepper. Put in a 2-quart casserole, top with the crumbs, and dot with butter. Bake for 35 to 40 minutes. Yield: 6 to 8 servings.

Spinach and Artichoke Casserole

2   14-ounce cans artichoke hearts
4   tablespoons garlic French salad dressing
3   10-ounce packages frozen chopped spinach

3   tablespoons butter
3   tablespoons all-purpose flour
1½ cups milk
¼   teaspoon salt
1   tablespoon Parmesan cheese

Marinate the artichokes in the dressing for several hours.

Preheat the oven to 375°. Grease a 2-quart casserole. Drain the artichokes, reserving the dressing, and put in the prepared casserole. Cook the spinach according to the package directions and drain. Make a white sauce: in a skillet melt the butter; add the flour and cook until bubbly; add the milk and salt and cook until it thickens, stirring constantly. Mix with the spinach and reserved dressing. Pour over the artichokes and top with the Parmesan cheese. Bake for 20 minutes. Yield: 6 to 8 servings.

Vegetable Casserole

1   small head cauliflower
8   small potatoes
8   small carrots
10 small onions
1   cup canned or frozen green peas

4   tablespoons butter
4   tablespoons all-purpose flour
2   cups milk
1   teaspoon salt
1   teaspoon pepper
½   pound sharp cheese, grated

Preheat the oven to 350°. Separate the cauliflower into flowerets and place in a large saucepan. Add the potatoes, carrots, and onions, and cook until tender. Drain well. Add the drained peas. Put in a 2-quart casserole. Make a white sauce: in a skillet melt the butter; add the flour and cook until bubbly; add the milk, salt, and pepper and cook until it thickens, stirring constantly. Add the cheese, and stir until melted. Pour over the vegetables. Bake uncovered to lightly brown the sauce, about 12 to 15 minutes. Yield: 8 servings.

Sweet Potatoes in Orange Cups

3 cups mashed cooked sweet potatoes
1 cup sugar
½ teaspoon salt
2 eggs
¼ cup butter
½ cup milk
1 teaspoon vanilla extract

Orange half shells, pulp removed

Topping
1 cup brown sugar
⅓ cup all-purpose flour
1 cup chopped nuts
¼ cup butter

Preheat the oven to 350°. In a large bowl mix together the sweet potatoes, sugar, salt, eggs, butter, milk, and vanilla. Pour into the orange halves. In a medium bowl mix together the brown sugar, flour, nuts, and butter, and sprinkle over the potato mixture in the orange cups. Bake for 35 minutes. Yield: 8 to 10 servings.

Herbed Tomatoes

6 large ripe tomatoes
1 teaspoon salt
¼ teaspoon black pepper
¼ cup finely snipped parsley

¼ cup chopped fresh or frozen chives
⅔ cup salad oil
¼ cup tarragon vinegar

Peel the tomatoes and cut in half crosswise. Place in a deep bowl, sprinkling each layer with seasonings and herbs. Combine the oil and vinegar and pour over the tomatoes. Cover and chill for an hour or more, basting often. Drain off the dressing and arrange the tomatoes on a platter. Yield: 12 servings. Yield: 12 servings.

Entrées

Beef Burgundy

2	tablespoons butter		Thyme
2	to 3 medium onions, sliced		Salt
2	pounds lean beef, cut into		Pepper
	1½ x ½-inch strips	½	cup beef bouillon
1½	tablespoons all-purpose flour	1	cup Burgundy wine
	Marjoram	½	pound sliced mushrooms

In a skillet heat the butter and sauté the onions. Transfer to a separate dish. In the same skillet brown the beef. Sprinkle with flour, marjoram, thyme, salt, and pepper. Add the bouillon and Burgundy. Stir well. Cover and simmer for 3 hours. The liquid seldom cooks away, but if it seems dry, add more bouillon and wine. Add the onions and mushrooms. Stir well. Cook for 1 hour longer. Yield: 6 to 8 servings.

Chicken Breasts in Wine

½	cup melted butter	1	cup heavy cream
1	green onion, chopped	1	cup sliced fresh mushrooms
4	large chicken breasts, split	1	teaspoon paprika
	Salt and pepper to taste		Sliced ripe olives
½	cup Marsala wine		

In a saucepan heat the butter and sauté the green onion. Add the chicken and cook until lightly browned. Add the salt and pepper to taste. Add the wine, cream, mushrooms, paprika, and olives. Cook, covered, until the chicken is tender, approximately 20 minutes. Yield: 4 or 8 servings.

Hot Baked Chicken Salad

2	cups chopped cooked chicken	½	teaspoon salt
2	cups chopped celery	2	tablespoons lemon juice
½	cup chopped pecans	2	teaspoons minced onion
1	cup salad dressing	½	cup grated cheese
		1	cup crumbled potato chips

Preheat the oven to 350°. In a large bowl combine the chicken, celery, nuts, salad dressing, salt, lemon juice, and onion. Pour into a greased casserole dish. In a small bowl mix the cheese and potato chips, and sprinkle over the casserole. Bake for 10 minutes. Yield: 6 to 8 servings.

Ham Casserole

2	cups chopped ham	1	tablespoon lemon juice
1	14-ounce can green asparagus	2	tablespoons uncooked tapioca
1	10¾-ounce can cream of mushroom soup	½	cup light cream
¼	cup grated cheese		Buttered breadcrumbs
2	tablespoons chopped onion		
2	tablespoons chopped green pepper		

Preheat the oven to 375°. In a 2-quart casserole dish arrange layers of ham and asparagus. In a large bowl mix the soup, cheese, onion, green pepper, lemon juice, tapioca, and cream, and pour over the ham and asparagus. Top with the buttered breadcrumbs. Bake for 30 minutes. Yield: 6 servings.

Creole Pork Chops

6	center-cut pork chops	1	8-ounce can tomato sauce
	Seasoned flour	1	small onion, chopped
	Salt, pepper, and paprika to	1	green pepper, chopped
	taste	½	cup sliced mushrooms
	Oil	¼	cup water
1	16-ounce can diced tomatoes		Cooked rice

Preheat the oven to 325°. Dredge the pork chops in the seasoned flour, salt, pepper, and paprika. In a skillet heat the oil and brown the pork chops. Place in a 2-quart casserole dish. Add the tomatoes, tomato sauce, onion, green pepper, mushrooms, and water. Cover. Bake for 1 hour and 30 minutes to 2 hours. Serve the pork chops and sauce with rice. Yield: 6 servings.

French Pot Roast

1	4-pound beef rump roast	1	stalk celery, diced
1	clove garlic	1	sprig parsley
¼	teaspoon pepper	1	bay leaf
1	teaspoon salt	1	sprig thyme
2	onions, sliced	2	cups dry red wine
3	tablespoons bacon drippings	1	cup tomato purée
2	carrots, sliced		

Preheat the oven to 350°. Rub the roast with garlic, pepper, and salt. In a skillet brown the onions in the bacon drippings. Remove and brown the roast on all sides. Add the carrots and celery, and brown. Transfer to a large ovenproof casserole dish with lid. Add the parsley, bay leaf, thyme, wine, and tomato purée. Cover and bake for 3 hours and 30 minutes. Add a small amount of hot water during baking if needed. Yield: 6 to 8 servings.

Steak Oriental

2 pounds lean steak, 1¼ to 1½ inches thick, cut into thin slices
Meat tenderizer
1 tablespoon salad oil
1 tablespoon gravy sauce
1 teaspoon salt
2 tablespoons soy sauce
3 beef bouillon cubes dissolved in 1 cup water
1 large onion, thinly sliced
2 cups celery, cut into long thin strips
1 8-ounce package frozen Chinese pea pods, thawed
1 tablespoon cornstarch dissolved in 2 tablespoons water
2 small red tomatoes, cut into wedges
4½ cups hot, fluffy rice with snipped parsley

Prepare the meat with the tenderizer according to the directions on the bottle. In a saucepan heat the salad oil and add the gravy sauce. Add the meat, stirring until brown. Add the salt, soy sauce, and bouillon. Simmer, covered, for 30 minutes or until fork tender. Add the onion and celery on top of the steak and cook over medium heat for 5 minutes. Add the thawed pea pods, and cook for 2 minutes. Thicken the liquid around the steak with the cornstarch mixture. Add the tomato wedges. Remove from the heat. Serve with hot rice. Yield: 8 servings.

Tuna Cashew Casserole

1 3-ounce can chow mein noodles
1 10¾-ounce can cream of mushroom soup
¼ cup water
1 6½-ounce can tuna
1 cup diced celery
¼ cup chopped ripe olives
¼ cup minced onion
½ teaspoon salt
½ teaspoon pepper
¼ cup chopped cashews

Preheat the oven to 350°. Grease a 1½-quart casserole dish. Set aside 1 cup noodles. In a large bowl combine the remaining noodles, soup, water, tuna, celery, olives, onion, salt, and pepper. Pour into the prepared casserole dish. Sprinkle with the reserved noodles and cashews just before baking. Bake for 40 minutes. Yield: 4 to 6 servings.

Parmesan Round Steak

1½	pounds round steak, cut ¾ inch thick	1	tablespoon Accent seasoning
1	egg, beaten	3	tablespoons bacon drippings
⅓	cup milk	½	cup water
½	cup fine dry breadcrumbs	¼	teaspoon leaf oregano
1¼	teaspoons salt	¼	cup grated Parmesan cheese
⅛	teaspoon pepper	¼	teaspoon paprika
		6	small onions

Preheat the oven to 325°. Cut the steak into 6 serving pieces. Pound to ½-inch thickness. In a shallow dish combine the egg and milk. In another dish mix the breadcrumbs, 1 teaspoon salt, the pepper, and Accent. Dip the steaks in the egg mixture and dredge with the seasoned crumbs. In a skillet heat the bacon drippings and brown the meat. Place the steaks in a casserole dish. Add water. Sprinkle with oregano. Place 2 teaspoons Parmesan cheese on each steak. Combine ¼ teaspoon salt and paprika. Sprinkle the onions with the salt mixture. Add to the meat, cover tightly. Bake for 1 hour and 30 minutes to 2 hours. Yield: 6 servings.

Sausage Casserole

1	pound ground pork sausage	1	green pepper, chopped
2	envelopes chicken noodle soup	1	medium onion, chopped
½	cup uncooked rice	½	cup chopped celery
4½	cups boiling water	½	cup slivered almonds

Preheat the oven to 350°. In a skillet brown the sausage, drain, and set aside. In a covered saucepan cook the soup mix and rice in the boiling water for 7 minutes. In a baking dish combine the sausage, rice mixture, and the remaining ingredients. (If desired, this dish can be prepared a day ahead and refrigerated.) Bake for 1 hour. This is delicious served with mushroom gravy. Yield: 8 to 10 servings.

Seafood and Rice Casserole

1¼ cups cooked rice
1 cup salad dressing
1 cup canned crabmeat
1 cup canned shrimp
1 small can mushrooms
5 tablespoons chopped onion

3 tablespoons Worcestershire
   sauce
1 green pepper, chopped
   Salt and pepper
   Slivered almonds

Preheat the oven to 350°. In a saucepan cook the rice. Add the salad dressing while the rice is still hot. Combine with the remaining ingredients and place in a casserole, topping with the slivered almonds. Bake for 30 minutes. This dish can be made ahead and frozen, but allow it to come to room temperature before baking. Yield: 6 servings.

Veal Parmesan

1 pound veal, thinly sliced
2 eggs, beaten
1 cup breadcrumbs
¼ cup cooking oil
1 10¾-ounce can condensed
   tomato soup
½ soup can water

¼ cup minced onion
1 clove garlic, minced
⅛ teaspoon thyme
4 ounces mozzarella cheese,
   thinly sliced
   Grated Parmesan cheese

Preheat the oven to 350°. Cut the veal into serving-sized pieces. Dip into the eggs and then into the breadcrumbs. In a skillet heat the oil and brown the veal. Place in a baking dish. Add the soup, water, onion, garlic, and thyme. Cook for 1 hour and 30 minutes. Top with the mozzarella cheese and sprinkle with the grated Parmesan cheese. Broil until the cheese melts. Yield: 6 servings.

Brunswick Stew

1	6-pound baking hen	2	packages frozen lima beans
2	pounds chicken breasts	2	16-ounce cans corn
3	quarts water	½	cup shredded cabbage
2	bay leaves	2	tablespoons sugar
4	small onions, finely chopped	1	tablespoon Worcestershire sauce
3	teaspoons salt		
1	teaspoon black pepper	1	teaspoon hot sauce
1	teaspoon red pepper	3	medium potatoes, diced
2	packages frozen sliced okra		
4	cups fresh or 2 (16 ounces each) cans diced tomatoes		

Cut the chicken into pieces. In a stockpot simmer the chicken in 3 quarts of water seasoned with bay leaves, onions, salt, black pepper, and red pepper, until the meat can be easily removed from the bones—about 2 hours and 30 minutes. Remove the chicken, dice, and set aside. Add the okra, tomatoes, lima beans, corn, cabbage, sugar, Worcestershire sauce, and hot sauce to the broth and cook slowly for 6 hours. Add the diced chicken, and cook for another hour. Thirty minutes before serving add the potatoes and cook until the potatoes are tender in the stew. This stew benefits from slow cooking. Its flavor improves if it is refrigerated overnight and then reheated. Yield: 12 to 16 servings.

Breads

Angel Biscuits

3 cups self-rising flour	1 cup buttermilk
1 tablespoon sugar	1 cake yeast, dissolved in ¼
½ teaspoon baking soda	cup warm water
1 cup shortening	

Preheat the oven to 425°. Grease a baking sheet. Into a large bowl sift together the dry ingredients, and cut in the shortening. Add the buttermilk and yeast mixture to make a soft dough. Turn out and knead for about 20 strokes. Roll to ¾-inch thickness. Cut the biscuits and cook on the prepared baking sheet for 15 minutes. Yield: 12 biscuits.

Buttermilk Banana Bread

½ cup butter	4 tablespoons buttermilk
1 cup sugar	2 cups all-purpose flour
3 ripe bananas	⅛ teaspoon salt
2 eggs	½ cup chopped walnuts
1 teaspoon baking soda	

Preheat the oven to 350°. Grease and flour 1 large loaf pan or 2 small loaf pans. In a large bowl mix the butter and sugar until soft using an electric mixer. Add the bananas and mix well. Add the eggs and continue mixing. In a small bowl dissolve the soda in the buttermilk. Add to the banana mixture. Add the flour and salt. Fold in the nuts. Bake in the prepared pan(s) for 1 hour. Yield: 1 large or 2 small loaves.

Cheese Drop Biscuits

2	cups grated sharp cheese	1	tablespoon salt
¼	cup shortening	¼	teaspoon cayenne pepper
2	eggs, well beaten	½	cup water
2	cups all-purpose flour, sifted		
3	tablespoons baking powder		

Preheat the oven to 425°. Grease a cookie sheet. In a large bowl mix the cheese, shortening, and eggs. Add the remaining ingredients, blending thoroughly. Drop balls of dough the size of small walnuts onto the prepared cookie sheet. Bake for about 15 minutes or until golden brown. Yield: 5 dozen.

Chocolate Date Bread

4	cups all-purpose flour, sifted	2	cups strong coffee
2½	tablespoons baking powder	¼	teaspoon baking soda
2	teaspoons salt	2	eggs, well beaten
1	cup sugar	¼	cup vegetable oil
1	cup chopped dates		
2	6-ounce packages semisweet chocolate morsels		

Preheat the oven to 375°. Grease and flour a 9 x 5 x 3-inch pan. Into a large bowl sift together the flour, baking powder, salt, and sugar. Add the dates and chocolate chips. Blend together well. Stir in the coffee, soda, eggs, and vegetable oil. Pour into the prepared pan. Bake for 1 hour. Yield: 1 loaf.

Quick Light Bread

1 cup boiling water	¼ cup lukewarm water
½ teaspoon salt	1 teaspoon sugar
2 tablespoons shortening	1 egg
¼ cup sugar	4 cups all-purpose flour
1 package dry yeast	

Preheat the oven to 425°. In a large bowl mix the water, salt, shortening, and sugar. Cool to lukewarm. Dissolve the yeast and 1 teaspoon sugar in ¼ cup lukewarm water, and add to the dough. Add the egg and 2 cups flour, beat well, and add the remaining flour until moistened. Don't knead. Let rise until double in bulk, about 1 hour. Shape into rolls or a loaf. Place in a warm place for about 1 hour to rise. Bake for 15 to 20 minutes for rolls or 25 to 30 minutes for a loaf. Yield: 1 loaf or 12 to 15 rolls.

Corn Light Bread

2 cups meal	1 teaspoon salt
¾ cup sugar	2 cups buttermilk
½ cup all-purpose flour	3 tablespoons shortening, melted
¼ teaspoon baking soda	

Preheat the oven to 350°. Grease a loaf pan. In a large bowl combine the dry ingredients and mix with the buttermilk and melted shortening. Bake in the prepared loaf pan for 1 hour until golden brown. Turn out on a rack and cool. Yield: 1 loaf.

Parmesan Cheese Biscuits

1 12-ounce can refrigerated biscuits	½ cup butter, melted Parmesan cheese

Dip the biscuits in the butter and sprinkle with Parmesan cheese. Stack in a slanted position, biscuits touching, in a loaf pan. Bake according to the package directions. Yield: 12 biscuits.

Cranberry Tea Bread

3 cups all-purpose flour	¾ cup water
1 teaspoon salt	½ cup orange juice
½ teaspoon soda	1 teaspoon grated orange rind
3 teaspoons baking powder	1 cup chopped nuts
½ cup margarine, melted	1½ cups cranberries, cut into
1½ cups sugar	halves or coarsely chopped
2 eggs	

Preheat the oven to 350°. Grease a 9 x 5-inch loaf pan. In a large bowl sift together the flour, salt, soda, and baking powder. In a separate bowl mix the margarine and sugar until soft. Add the eggs and mix well. In a medium bowl combine the water, orange juice, and orange rind, and add to the egg mixture alternately with the sifted dry ingredients. Fold in the nuts and cranberries. Pour into the prepared pan. Bake for 1 hour. Turn out onto a rack to cool. This bread slices better the second day and freezes so well it can be made weeks ahead. Yield: 1 loaf.

Lemon Muffins

1 cup butter	1 teaspoon salt
1 cup sugar	½ cup lemon juice
4 egg yolks, well beaten	4 egg whites, stiffly beaten
2 cups all-purpose flour	1 tablespoon grated lemon
2 teaspoons baking powder	peel

Preheat the oven to 375°. Butter the cups of a muffin pan. In a mixing bowl mix the butter and sugar until smooth. Add the egg yolks and beat until light. Into a separate bowl sift the flour, baking powder, and salt. Add the dry ingredients alternately with the lemon juice, mixing thoroughly after each addition. Fold in the stiffly beaten egg whites and grated lemon peel. Fill the prepared muffin cups and bake for about 20 minutes. These freeze well and are good split and toasted with salads. Yield: 12 to 15 muffins.

Fudge Muffins

1   cup margarine
4   1-ounce squares semisweet
    chocolate
1   cup sugar
½   teaspoon salt

1   cup all-purpose flour
4   eggs
1   teaspoon vanilla extract
2   cups chopped walnuts

Preheat the oven to 325°. Grease the cups of a muffin pan. In a saucepan melt the margarine and chocolate. Beat in the sugar, salt, and flour. Then add the eggs one at a time, stirring in. Add the vanilla and chopped walnuts. Pour into the prepared muffin pan and bake for 25 minutes. Yield: 12 large or 24 small muffins.

Tropical Muffins

1¾ cups sifted all-purpose flour
½   cup sugar
2   teaspoons baking powder
¼   teaspoon baking soda
¾   teaspoon salt
½   cup coconut

⅓   cup shortening, melted
1   egg, beaten
1   cup mashed ripe bananas
⅓   cup orange juice
1   teaspoon grated orange rind

Preheat the oven to 375°. Butter the cups of a muffin pan. Into a medium bowl sift together the dry ingredients. Add the coconut. In a separate bowl combine the shortening, egg, bananas, orange juice, and orange rind. Add to the dry ingredients. Stir quickly with a fork only until the dry ingredients are moistened. Bake in the prepared pan for 25 to 30 minutes. Yield: 12 to 18 muffins.

Recipes from Miss Daisy's

Pineapple Surprise

½ cup margarine	1 16-ounce can crushed
3 eggs, beaten	pineapple
½ cup sugar	5 slices bread, cubed

Preheat the oven to 350°. In a small bowl mix the margarine, eggs, sugar, and pineapple. Place the bread cubes in a casserole dish and stir in the pineapple mixture. Bake, covered, for 40 minutes. Cut into squares. This is especially good with ham. Yield: 6 servings.

Refrigerator Potato Rolls

1 cake yeast	1 cup mashed Irish potatoes
½ cup lukewarm water	1 cup milk, scalded
⅔ cup shortening	2 eggs, well beaten
½ cup sugar	5½ to 6 cups all-purpose flour,
1 teaspoon salt	sifted

Dissolve the yeast in the lukewarm water. In a large bowl mix the shortening, sugar, salt, and mashed potatoes. Add the scalded milk. Cool to room temperature. Add the yeast and eggs. Gradually add the flour and mix well. Form to the desired number of rolls and let rise to double bulk.

Preheat the oven to 400°. Bake the rolls for 15 to 20 minutes. Cover and refrigerate the remaining dough. Use as needed. Let rise before baking. Yield: 5 dozen rolls.

Apple Crisp

4 cups sliced tart apples	1 cup white or brown sugar
½ cup water	1 teaspoon ground cinnamon
2 tablespoons lemon juice	½ cup butter
¾ cup all-purpose flour	

Preheat the oven to 350°. Arrange the apples in a buttered baking dish. Pour the water and lemon juice over the apples. In a bowl blend the flour, sugar, cinnamon, and butter with a pastry blender. Sprinkle this mixture on top of the apples. Bake for 30 minutes. Serve warm with ice cream. Yield: 6 servings.

Chocolate Tarts

2 1-ounce squares unsweetened chocolate	½ teaspoon salt
	3 egg yolks
2 cups milk	1 tablespoon butter
1 cup sugar	1 teaspoon vanilla extract
⅓ cup all-purpose flour	8 cooked tart shells

In a saucepan melt the chocolate and milk over low heat. In a small bowl mix the sugar, flour, and salt, and add enough chocolate mixture to make a paste. Slowly add this mixture back to the chocolate mixture. Cook over low to medium heat, stirring constantly, until thick. In a medium bowl beat the egg yolks and slowly add to the mixture. Cook slowly for 1 minute, then add the butter and vanilla. Cool and fill cooked tart shells. This recipe also makes a delicious chocolate pie. Yield: 6 to 8 servings.

Crème de Menthe Party Dessert

55 large marshmallows	40 double lady fingers
1 cup real crème de menthe	Whipped cream
2 cups heavy cream	Shaved bitter chocolate

In a double boiler dissolve the marshmallows in the crème de menthe. Let cool. In a medium bowl beat the cream and fold it into the mixture. Line 2 8-inch square pans with crossed pieces of wax paper. Line the sides and bottom with opened lady fingers. Alternate layers of lady fingers with the crème de menthe mixture, ending with the crème de menthe mixture. Top with whipped cream and sprinkle with shaved bitter chocolate. Lift from the pan with the wax paper. Refrigerate. Yield: 18 servings.

Fat Man's Misery

14 chocolate cream cookies	2 cups heavy cream
½ cup butter	½ tablespoon sugar
1 cup confectioners' sugar	1 teaspoon vanilla extract
1 egg	1 cup chopped pecans
Few drops almond flavoring	

Crush the cookies. Line a 9-inch pie pan or square pan with most of the crushed cookies, saving some for the topping. In a mixing bowl mix the butter and sugar until soft. Add the egg, and cream again. Add the almond flavoring. Spread this mixture over the crumbs. In a separate bowl whip the cream with the sugar. Add the vanilla and pecans. Fold until well blended. Spread this over the first mixture. Cover with the reserved crushed cookies. Let stand in the refrigerator for 24 hours. Yield: 6 to 9 servings.

Hello Dollies

½ cup butter, melted
1 cup finely crushed graham cracker crumbs
1 cup flaked coconut
1 cup chocolate morsels
1 cup chopped nuts
1 14-ounce can sweetened condensed milk

Preheat the oven to 350°. In a small bowl mix the butter and graham cracker crumbs, and place in a 9-inch square pan. Layer first the coconut, then the chocolate morsels, and then the chopped nuts in the pan. Pour the sweetened condensed milk over the mixture and smooth it out evenly. Bake for 25 to 30 minutes. Let cool in the pan and cut into small squares—these are very rich. Yield: 12 servings.

Peach Cobbler

2 cups sliced fresh peaches (or canned if desired)
2 cups sugar
½ cup butter
¾ cup all-purpose flour
2 teaspoons baking powder
¼ teaspoon salt
¾ cup milk

Preheat the oven to 325°. In a medium bowl mix the peaches with 1 cup sugar. Set aside. Put the butter in a 2-quart casserole, and place in the oven to melt. In a large bowl combine the remaining sugar, flour, baking powder, salt, and milk. Pour over the melted butter. Do not stir. Spoon the peaches on top of the batter. Do not stir. Bake for 1 hour. Yield: 6 servings.

Lemon Squares

1	cup all-purpose flour	½	teaspoon salt
¼	cup confectioners' sugar	1	teaspoon baking powder
½	cup butter	2	eggs
1	cup sugar	4	tablespoons lemon juice

Preheat the oven to 350°. In a mixing bowl mix the flour, confectioners' sugar, and butter until soft, and press evenly into the bottom of a 9-inch square pan. Bake for 20 minutes. Beat together the sugar, salt, baking powder, eggs, and lemon juice. Pour over the hot crust and bake for 20 to 25 minutes until no imprint remains when touched lightly. Cool and cut into 2-inch squares. You may want to sprinkle with confectioners' sugar. Yield: 6 to 9 servings.

Fresh Apple Cake

1½	cups salad oil	1	teaspoon salt
2	cups sugar	1	teaspoon baking soda
3	eggs	1	cup nuts (I use walnuts)
2½	cups all-purpose flour	1	teaspoon vanilla extract
2	teaspoons baking powder	3	cups chopped tart apples

In a mixing bowl cream together the oil, sugar, and eggs. Into a large bowl sift the dry ingredients, and mix gradually into the creamed mixture. Fold in the nuts, vanilla, and apples. Bake in a tube pan for 1 hour at 350° or in 2 loaf pans for 1 hour at 300°. Reduce the heat to 250° until done. Yield: 15 to 18 servings.

Kentucky Butter Cake

3	cups cake flour, sifted	2	cups sugar
1	teaspoon baking powder	4	eggs, unbeaten
1	teaspoon salt	1	cup buttermilk
½	teaspoon baking soda	2	teaspoons rum flavoring
1	cup butter		Sauce (see below)

Preheat the oven to 325°. Into a mixing bowl sift together the flour, baking powder, salt, and soda. In a separate bowl mix the butter and sugar until soft. Blend in the unbeaten eggs one at a time, beating well after each addition. In another bowl combine the buttermilk and rum flavoring, and add to the butter mixture alternately with the dry ingredients, blending well after each addition. Turn into a tube pan. Bake for 1 hour to 1 hour and 15 minutes. Prick with a fork. Pour hot sauce over the cake. Cool before removing from the pan. Yield: 16 servings.

Sauce for Kentucky Butter Cake

1	cup sugar	½	cup butter
¼	cup water	2	tablespoons rum flavoring

In a saucepan heat the sugar, water, and butter until melted. Add 2 tablespoons rum flavoring. Pour over hot Kentucky Butter Cake.

2	cups all-purpose flour
2	cups sugar
½	cup shortening
½	cup margarine
1	cup water
3	tablespoons cocoa
2	eggs, slightly beaten
½	cup buttermilk
1	teaspoon baking soda
2	teaspoons vanilla extract

Icing

½	cup butter
3	tablespoons cocoa
6	tablespoons milk
1	1-pound box confectioners' sugar
1	cup chopped pecans or walnuts
2	teaspoons vanilla extract

Preheat the oven to 350°. Grease and flour an 11 x 16-inch pan. In a mixing bowl combine the flour and sugar. In a saucepan combine the shortening, margarine, water, and cocoa. Bring to a boil and pour over the flour-sugar mixture. Add the eggs, buttermilk, soda, and vanilla. Mix well, and pour into the prepared pan. Bake for 25 minutes.

To make the icing, in a saucepan combine the butter, cocoa, and milk, and bring to a boil. Add the confectioners' sugar and beat until smooth. Add the nuts and vanilla. Spread over the hot cake. This is excellent cut into 1-inch squares for morning coffees or afternoon teas. Yield: 24 squares.

Skillet Coffee Cake

¾ cup butter or margarine
1½ cups sugar
2 eggs
1½ cups sifted all-purpose flour

½ teaspoon salt
1 teaspoon almond flavoring
Slivered almonds
Sugar

Preheat the oven to 350°. Line a large iron skillet with aluminum foil, leaving excess foil on either side. Set aside. In a saucepan melt the butter. In a mixing bowl combine the melted butter and the sugar. Beat in the eggs one at a time. Add the flour, salt, and almond flavoring, and mix well. Pour the batter into the prepared iron skillet. Cover the top with slivered almonds and sprinkle with granulated sugar. Bake for 30 to 40 minutes. Remove the cake from the pan using the foil, and when cool, wrap tightly in the foil to store. Do not try to peel the foil while the cake is still warm; it will stick. This is a very rich coffee cake, so serve it in small pieces. Yield: 6 to 8 servings.

Angel Cake–Chocolate Sauce

2 6-ounce packages semisweet chocolate morsels
2½ tablespoons water
2 eggs, separated
2 tablespoons confectioners' sugar

1 cup whipped cream
½ cup chopped nuts
1 angel food cake

In a double boiler melt the chocolate with the water. Add the egg yolks one at a time. Beat well. In a medium bowl beat the egg whites until stiff and add the confectioners' sugar. Add the whipped cream and chopped nuts. Gently fold the egg white mixture into the chocolate mixture. Break the angel food cake into small pieces and put in a Pyrex dish. Pour half of the sauce over the cake and repeat layers. Chill in the refrigerator for 24 hours. Cut into squares and top with whipped cream. Yield: 12 servings.

Rum Cake

1 18.25-ounce package yellow
   cake mix
1 3-ounce package instant
   vanilla pudding
4 eggs
1 cup salad oil
1 cup water

1 teaspoon vanilla extract
2 teaspoons rum flavoring
Sauce
1 cup sugar
½ cup water
1 teaspoon vanilla extract
2 teaspoons rum flavoring

Preheat the oven to 350°. Generously butter a tube pan. In a mixing bowl combine all of the ingredients and beat for 10 minutes. Pour into the prepared pan. Bake for 45 minutes. To make the sauce, in a saucepan combine the sugar and water, and boil for 3 minutes. Add the vanilla and rum flavoring and pour over the cake while still warm. (This is my favorite Rum Cake recipe.) Yield: 15 to 18 servings.

Pound Cake

1 cup butter
½ cup shortening
3 cups sugar
5 eggs
1 cup milk

3 cups all-purpose flour
½ teaspoon baking powder
1 teaspoon vanilla extract
1 teaspoon lemon extract

Preheat the oven to 350°. In a mixing bowl mix the butter, shortening, and sugar until soft. Add the eggs one at a time. Add the milk alternately with the flour and baking powder. Stir in the vanilla and lemon extracts and pour into a 10-inch tube pan. Bake for 1 hour, then reduce the oven temperature to 325° and bake for 15 minutes or until the cake tests done. Yield: 12 to 15 servings.

Orange Pound Cake

1   18.25-ounce package yellow cake mix

4   eggs

⅔   cup salad oil

1   3-ounce package orange gelatin

¾   cup orange juice concentrate

Sauce

1   cup orange juice

1   cup confectioners' sugar

Preheat the oven to 325°. In a mixing bowl combine the cake mix, eggs, oil, gelatin, and orange juice concentrate, and beat for 5 minutes. Bake in a tube pan for 45 minutes. Turn out on a rack and while cooling make the sauce. In a saucepan cook the orange juice and sugar until dissolved and bubbling. (3 to 5 minutes). While the sauce is still hot spoon it over the cake. Yield: 12 to 15 servings.

Fudge Cake

1   cup butter

4   1-ounce squares bittersweet chocolate

4   eggs

2   cups sugar

1   cup all-purpose flour

1   teaspoon vanilla extract

1   cup chopped nuts

Icing

½   cup butter

2   ounces unsweetened chocolate

1   1-pound box confectioners' sugar

5   tablespoons evaporated milk

1   teaspoon vanilla extract

Preheat the oven to 275°. Grease and flour 2 8-inch square pans. In a saucepan melt 1 cup butter and the bittersweet chocolate over low heat. In a large bowl mix the eggs and sugar and add the flour. Add the chocolate mixture, 1 teaspoon vanilla, and nuts to the flour mixture and mix well. Pour into the prepared pans. Bake for 45 to 50 minutes.

To make the icing, in a saucepan melt ½ cup butter and the unsweetened chocolate. Add the confectioners' sugar, evaporated milk, and 1 teaspoon vanilla. Mix until creamy. Ice the cooled cake. Yield: 12 to 16 servings.

Strawberry Angel Food Cake

1   angel food cake
1   large package frozen
    strawberries, drained
1   8-ounce can crushed
    pineapple, drained
16 marshmallows, cut up
½   teaspoon vanilla extract
4   cups whipped topping

Cut the cake into 3 layers. In a large bowl combine the strawberries, pineapple, marshmallows, vanilla, and whipped topping. Ice the cake with this mixture, spreading carefully between the layers and reassembling the cake. Keep in the refrigerator after iced. Yield: 12 to 15 servings.

Chocolate Chip-Almond Pie

6   small chocolate bars with
    almonds
17 marshmallows
½   cup milk
1   cup heavy cream, whipped
½   cup chocolate chips
½   cup slivered almonds
1   baked graham cracker crust
    Shaved chocolate for garnish

In a double boiler melt the chocolate bars and marshmallows with the milk. Cool. Fold in the whipped cream, chocolate chips, and slivered almonds. Pour into the graham cracker crust. Garnish with shaved chocolate. Refrigerate for at least 4 hours before serving. Yield: 6 servings.

Peanut Butter Ice Cream Pie

4 tablespoons peanut butter
4 tablespoons light brown sugar

1 pint vanilla ice cream
1 graham cracker crust
Crushed peanuts

In a saucepan melt the peanut butter and brown sugar. Add the ice cream and stir until the mixture is well blended. Pour into the graham cracker crust. Sprinkle crushed peanuts on top. Freeze. Yield: 6 servings.

Grasshopper Pie with Chocolate Wafer Crust

24 marshmallows
½ cup milk
¼ cup crème de menthe

1 cup heavy cream
1 9-inch chocolate wafer crust (see below)

In a saucepan melt the marshmallows in the milk. Let cool. Add the crème de menthe. Whip the cream and fold it into the mixture. Pour into the crust and refrigerate. Yield: 6 servings.

Chocolate Wafer Crust

¾ cup chocolate cookie crumbs

2 tablespoons butter, melted

Combine the crumbs and butter and press into the bottom and sides of a 9-inch pan.

Millionaire Pie

2 cups confectioners' sugar
¼ cup butter
2 eggs
1 teaspoon vanilla extract
2 9-inch baked pie shells
1 cup heavy cream
2½ tablespoons confectioners' sugar

½ teaspoon plain gelatin
1 1-pound can crushed pineapple, drained
½ cup maraschino cherries, chopped
¼ cup chopped pecans

In a large bowl mix 2 cups confectioners' sugar, the butter, eggs, and vanilla. Spread evenly in the baked pie shells. Refrigerate. In a large bowl whip the cream, 2½ tablespoons sugar, and gelatin. Fold the drained pineapple, cherries, and nuts into the whipped cream mixture. Top the pies with this mixture and refrigerate. Yield: 12 to 16 servings.

Buttermilk Raisin Pie

1 cup buttermilk
1 cup sugar
1 cup raisins
1 tablespoon butter
½ teaspoon salt

½ teaspoon ground cinnamon
1 egg, beaten
½ teaspoon vanilla extract
Unbaked pie shell; pie crust strips

Preheat the oven to 325°. In a saucepan combine the buttermilk, sugar, raisins, butter, salt, cinnamon, and egg. Bring to a boil. Boil for 1 minute. Let cool and add the vanilla. Pour into an unbaked pie shell. Top with pie crust strips and bake for 30 to 40 minutes. Yield: 6 servings.

Rum Cream Pie

1 envelope unflavored gelatin	1½ cups heavy cream
5 egg yolks	Crumb Crust (see below)
1 cup sugar	Unsweetened chocolate
⅓ cup dark rum	

In a saucepan soften the gelatin in ½ cup cold water. Place over low heat and bring almost to a boil, stirring to dissolve. In a mixing bowl beat the egg yolks and sugar until very light. Stir the gelatin into the egg mixture, and cool. Gradually add the rum, beating constantly. In a separate bowl whip the cream until it stands in soft peaks and fold into the gelatin mixture. Cool until the mixture begins to set, then spoon into the crumb crust and chill until firm enough to cut. Grate unsweetened chocolate over the top before serving. Yield: 6 to 8 servings.

Crumb Crust

2¼ cups graham cracker crumbs	2 tablespoons sugar
½ cup melted butter	1 teaspoon ground cinnamon

Combine the ingredients and press into the bottom and sides of a 9-inch pie pan. Chill.

Cornmeal Pie

1½ cups sugar
1½ cups packed dark brown
    sugar
½ cup butter, melted
3 eggs, separated
1½ teaspoons vanilla extract

½ cup light cream
½ cup cornmeal
½ cup chopped pecans
½ cup coconut
1 unbaked 10-inch pie crust

Preheat the oven to 350°. In a large bowl blend the sugars and butter. Add the beaten egg yolks, vanilla, cream, and cornmeal. Add the pecans and coconut. Add the lightly beaten egg whites, and blend. Bake for 35 minutes. Yield: 6 servings.

Coconut Ice Box Pie

1 cup sugar
2 tablespoons all-purpose flour
1 cup milk
1 egg, slightly beaten
1 teaspoon vanilla extract

Small package frozen fresh
coconut
Prebaked pie shell
Whipped cream for topping

In a saucepan combine the sugar, flour, milk, and egg, and cook until thick. Add the vanilla and ½ package of coconut. Pour into the pie shell. Top with whipped cream and sprinkle with the remaining coconut. Refrigerate until ready to serve. Yield: 6 servings.

12 saltines, crushed
12 dates, chopped
½ cup chopped pecans
1 cup sugar
¼ teaspoon baking powder
3 egg whites, beaten stiff but not dry
1 teaspoon almond extract

Preheat the oven to 350°. In a large bowl mix together the crackers, dates, pecans, sugar, and baking powder. Fold in the egg whites and extract. Pour into a buttered pie plate. Bake for 30 minutes. Yield: 6 servings.

Springtime Torte

1	18.25-ounce box yellow cake mix	4	eggs, separated
⅓	cup water	¼	teaspoon cream of tartar
1	cup orange juice	1	cup sugar
1	teaspoon grated orange rind	2	cups heavy cream

Preheat the oven to 350°. Grease 2 9-inch cake pans and line with wax paper. In a large bowl combine the cake mix, water, orange juice, orange rind, and egg yolks, and beat with an electric mixer for 4 minutes on medium speed. Pour into the prepared pans. In a separate bowl beat the egg whites with the cream of tartar and sugar until stiff. Spoon the meringue over the torte. Bake for 40 minutes. Cool completely before removing from the pans. Whip the heavy cream and sweeten to taste. Frost the torte with the whipped cream. Refrigerate. Serve with sweetened fresh strawberries. Yield: 6 to 8 servings.

Banana Pineapple Cake

3	cups all-purpose flour	1½	cups salad oil
2	cups sugar	3	eggs
1	teaspoon baking soda	1½	teaspoons vanilla extract
1	teaspoon salt	2	cups diced bananas
1	teaspoon ground cinnamon		
1	8-ounce can crushed pineapple with juice		

Preheat the oven to 350°. In a large bowl mix all ingredients together (do not use a mixer). Pour into a greased and floured tube pan. Bake at least 1 hour and 20 minutes. Cool completely before removing from the pan. Yield: 12 to 15 servings.

Sunday Down South

At one time the Tearoom offered the Sunday Down South Buffet. It was reminiscent of a traditional Sunday meal in the Old South when families gathered at home for a huge meal after church. The buffet was sinfully laden with varied and tempting foods.

The menu changed weekly as well as seasonally to ensure freshness and variety. Each Sunday meal included seven salads; freshly baked bread; homemade desserts; and the grand dame of the South, fried chicken. Also, the buffet boasted enticing vegetable casseroles, which are rarely included in restaurant fare. These became something of a specialty. Based on the premise that simplicity is often a characteristic of delicious food, the following recipes are not complicated, just delicious.

Amid the sound of splashing water, lush greenery, and fresh air, courtyard dining was available on lazy spring, summer, or fall afternoons. At times, there was a strolling musician to please old and young alike.

Sunday Down South was more than just having lunch. You could enjoy meandering to the front lawn of Carter's Court where, weather permitting, there was some type of family entertainment. Guests sat on church pews and enjoyed not only the tranquillity but the lingering atmosphere of a traditional Sunday Down South. The afternoon was sure to satisfy anyone's longing to escape the chaos of the modern world and return to a more leisurely pace.

Salads

Strawberry-Lemon Congealed Salad

1 3-ounce package strawberry
   gelatin
2 cups boiling water
1 21-ounce can strawberry pie
   filling
1 3-ounce package lemon
   gelatin

⅓ cup mayonnaise
1 3-ounce package cream
   cheese
1 8¾-ounce can crushed
   pineapple, drained
½ cup heavy cream, whipped

In a heatproof bowl dissolve the strawberry gelatin in 1 cup boiling water. Stir in the pie filling. Pour into a 9 x 9-inch dish; chill until partially set. In a separate heatproof bowl dissolve the lemon gelatin in 1 cup boiling water. In a medium bowl beat the mayonnaise and cream cheese using an electric mixer. Beat in the lemon gelatin. Fold in the pineapple and whipped cream. Spread on the strawberry layer. Chill. Cut into squares to serve. Yield: 6 to 9 servings.

Congealed Spiced Peach Salad

1 16-ounce can sliced peaches
¼ cup vinegar
½ cup sugar
12 whole cloves

⅛ teaspoon ground cinnamon
1 3-ounce package orange
   gelatin
¾ cup cold water

Drain the peaches, reserving 1 cup syrup. Chop the peaches coarsely. In a saucepan bring the syrup, vinegar, sugar, cloves, and cinnamon to a boil and simmer for 10 minutes. Strain the syrup and discard the cloves. Dissolve the gelatin in the hot syrup. Add the cold water and peaches. Chill until slightly thickened. Pour into a mold or a 9 x 9-inch dish. Congeal. Yield: 6 to 9 servings.

Christmas Ribbon Salad

1 6-ounce package lime gelatin
1 6-ounce package raspberry
  gelatin
1 3-ounce package lemon
  gelatin
5 cups boiling water
1 cup miniature marshmallows

3 cups cold water
6 ounces cream cheese,
  softened
½ cup mayonnaise
1 cup heavy cream, whipped
1 20½-ounce can crushed
  pineapple, drained

Dissolve the gelatin flavors separately, using 2 cups boiling water each for the lime and raspberry gelatins; 1 cup boiling water for the lemon gelatin. Stir the marshmallows into the lemon gelatin; set aside. Add 1½ cups cold water to the lime gelatin and pour into a 9 x 13-inch dish. Chill until set, but not firm. Meanwhile, add 1½ cups cold water to the raspberry gelatin and set aside at room temperature. Add the cream cheese to the lemon mixture, and beat until blended. Chill until slightly thickened. Then blend in the mayonnaise, whipped cream, and crushed pineapple. Chill until thick, and spoon gently (do not pour) over the lime layer. Chill until set. Meanwhile, chill the raspberry gelatin until thickened. Spoon gently over the lemon layer. Chill until firm. Cut into squares and serve on a lettuce leaf. Yield: 12 servings.

Lime Fluff

1 3-ounce package lime gelatin
1 16-ounce carton cottage
  cheese
1 14-ounce can crushed
  pineapple, drained

1 6-ounce carton whipped
  topping

In a large bowl sprinkle the gelatin over the cottage cheese. Mix. Add the pineapple and whipped topping. Mix thoroughly. Chill until ready to serve. Yield: 6 servings.

Marinated Green Vegetables

1   16-ounce can small peas
1   16-ounce can cut green
    beans
1   can Chinese vegetables
1   cup chopped green pepper
½   cup chopped onion

1   4-ounce can chopped
    pimientos
1   cup white vinegar
1   cup sugar
1   cup vegetable oil

Drain the canned vegetables. In a large bowl mix all of the vegetables gently. In a medium bowl make a marinade of the vinegar, sugar, and oil. Pour over the vegetables. Refrigerate for 24 hours before serving. Yield: 12 to 16 servings.

Sauerkraut Salad

2   pounds sauerkraut
1   cup sugar
1   large onion, finely chopped
1   green pepper, finely
    chopped

1   cup finely chopped celery
1   2-ounce jar pimientos,
    chopped
½   cup vegetable oil
¼   cup wine vinegar

Drain the sauerkraut and place in a large bowl; add the sugar. Let the sugar and sauerkraut stand for 10 minutes. Drain off any liquid. In a separate bowl combine the onion, pepper, celery, and pimientos. In a small bowl mix the oil and vinegar. Pour over the vegetables. Add the sauerkraut and toss. Refrigerate for 24 hours before serving. Yield: 6 to 8 servings.

2	envelopes plain gelatin softened in ½ cup cold water	2	7-ounce cans white tuna, drained and mashed
1	cup mayonnaise	2	teaspoons horseradish, drained
2	tablespoons lemon juice		
1	cup chopped celery	½	teaspoon salt
½	cup chopped stuffed olives	¼	teaspoon hot sauce
2	tablespoons chopped chives	1	cup heavy cream, whipped
4	hard-boiled eggs, mashed		

In a saucepan heat the softened gelatin until dissolved. Add the mayonnaise and lemon juice. Mix with a wire whisk. Add the celery, olives, chives, eggs, tuna, horseradish, salt, and hot sauce. Mix thoroughly. Chill for about 1 hour. Fold in the whipped cream. Pour into a 9 x 9-inch dish. Cut into squares to serve. Yield: 6 servings.

Vegetables

Broccoli-Rice Casserole

2 cups cooked rice
2 10-ounce packages broccoli cuts, cooked and drained
8 ounces American processed cheese, cubed
1 10¾-ounce can cream of chicken soup

1 6-ounce can water chestnuts, drained and sliced
½ cup milk
1 teaspoon Worcestershire sauce
Salt and pepper to taste
Breadcrumbs

Preheat the oven to 350°. Butter a 2-quart casserole. In a large bowl combine the hot rice and broccoli with the American cheese. Allow the cheese to melt, then add the soup, water chestnuts, milk, Worcestershire sauce, salt, and pepper. Place in the prepared casserole. Sprinkle breadcrumbs on top. Bake for 20 to 30 minutes. Yield: 9 to 12 servings.

Asparagus and English Pea Casserole

1 16-ounce can peas
1 16-ounce can asparagus cuts
1 8-ounce can mushroom pieces

1 10¾-ounce can cream of mushroom soup
½ cup cracker crumbs
½ cup grated Cheddar cheese

Preheat the oven to 350°. Butter a 2-quart casserole. Drain the vegetables and mushroom pieces. Layer half of the peas, asparagus, mushroom pieces, soup, cracker crumbs, and Cheddar cheese in the prepared dish. Repeat the layers. Bake for 30 minutes. Yield: 9 to 12 servings.

Spinach and Tomato Bake

4 medium tomatoes	1 tablespoon chopped onion
1 10-ounce package frozen chopped spinach, thawed and well drained	1 egg, beaten
	¼ cup butter, melted
½ cup herb stuffing mix	¼ cup Parmesan cheese

Preheat the oven to 350°. Grease a baking dish. Slice each tomato into 2 thick slices. Let drain if they are watery. Place in the prepared baking dish in a single layer, sliced side facing up. In a bowl mix the remaining ingredients. Make mounds of the spinach mixture on each tomato slice. Bake for 15 minutes. Yield: 4 to 8 servings.

Rice Supreme

½ cup butter or margarine	1 10¾-ounce can cream of mushroom soup
1 cup long grain rice	
2 cups chopped celery	½ teaspoon curry powder
1 cup chopped onion	
1 10½-ounce can beef consommé	

Preheat the oven to 350°. Grease a 1½-quart baking dish. In a large skillet heat the butter and brown the rice, stirring often, over medium heat. Add the celery and onion and continue cooking for 5 minutes. Remove from the heat; add the consommé, soup, and curry powder. Mix well with a wire whisk. Pour the mixture into the prepared baking dish. Cover and bake for 1 hour. Yield: 6 to 8 servings.

Oriental Vegetable Casserole

1 16-ounce can French-style green beans
1 16-ounce can Chinese vegetables
2 10¾-ounce cans cream of mushroom soup
1 pound Cheddar cheese, grated
2 3-ounce cans Chinese noodles

Preheat the oven to 350°. Grease a 3-quart casserole dish. Drain the vegetables. Layer half of the beans, Chinese vegetables, soup, Cheddar cheese, and noodles in the prepared casserole. Repeat the layers. Bake for 30 minutes. Yield: 12 servings.

Easy Spinach Casserole

3 10-ounce packages frozen chopped spinach, thawed and well drained
1 package onion soup mix
½ cup butter, melted
½ teaspoon nutmeg

Preheat the oven to 350°. Butter a 2-quart casserole dish. In a large bowl mix the spinach, soup mix, butter, and nutmeg. Bake in the prepared casserole dish for 30 minutes. Yield: 6 to 8 servings.

Sweet Potato Pudding

4 cups grated or shredded raw sweet potatoes
2 cups sugar
1⅓ cups milk
4 eggs, beaten
½ heaping teaspoon ground allspice
½ heaping teaspoon ground cinnamon

Preheat the oven to 350°. Grease a shallow dish. Peel and grate the sweet potatoes, and combine with the remaining ingredients. Bake in the prepared dish for 1 hour. Yield: 6 to 8 servings.

Corn Pudding

2½ cups cream-style corn
5 tablespoons all-purpose flour
1 tablespoon sugar
1 teaspoon salt
¼ cup butter, melted
¾ cup milk
3 eggs, beaten

Preheat the oven to 325°. Butter a 1-quart casserole dish. In a large bowl mix the corn and flour with a wire whisk. Add the remaining ingredients and mix. Bake in the prepared dish for 1 hour. Yield: 6 servings. Yield: 6 servings.

Eggplant Casserole

2 large eggplants
3 medium onions, sliced
2 cups canned spaghetti sauce
1 cup mozzarella cheese
¼ cup grated Parmesan cheese

Preheat the oven to 350°. Grease a casserole dish. Peel and slice the eggplant into ½-inch slices. In a saucepan boil the eggplant slices in a small amount of water for 10 minutes. Layer the eggplant, onions, sauce, and mozzarella cheese in a greased casserole. Repeat the layers. Top with the Parmesan cheese. Bake for 45 minutes. Zucchini may be substituted for the eggplant. Do not peel, but slice and boil it the same way. Yield: 8 to 10 servings.

Carrot-Raisin Casserole

⅓ cup butter, softened	¾ cup raisins
½ cup sugar	¾ cup milk
3 eggs, beaten	¾ teaspoon baking powder
3 cups mashed cooked carrots	Grated rind of 1 lemon

Preheat the oven to 350°. Butter a 1-quart casserole dish. In a large bowl mix the butter and sugar until soft. Add the eggs and mix. Blend in the remaining ingredients. Bake in the prepared casserole dish for 30 minutes. Yield: 6 servings.

Quick and Easy Peas

2 16-ounce cans small English peas	1 10¾-ounce can cream of mushroom soup
¼ cup butter	Grated Cheddar cheese
¼ cup finely chopped onion	

Drain the peas. In a saucepan heat the butter and sauté the onion. Add the peas and soup. Heat and serve. You may also put this in a buttered 1-quart casserole, top with grated Cheddar cheese, and bake at 350° for 20 minutes. Yield: 6 servings.

Squash Casserole

3 pounds yellow squash or zucchini	1 10¾-ounce can cream of mushroom soup
1 onion, chopped	1 teaspoon salt
¼ cup butter	¾ teaspoon pepper
3 eggs, beaten	Cracker crumbs

Preheat the oven to 350°. Butter a 2-quart casserole dish. In a saucepan cook the squash and onion until tender. Drain well. Add the butter and mix well. Fold in the eggs, soup, salt, and pepper. Place in the prepared casserole dish and top with a thin layer of cracker crumbs. Bake for 30 minutes. Yield: 8 to 10 servings.

Recipes from Miss Daisy's

Sweet and Sour Chicken

1   3- to 4-pound fryer or 8 split breasts
1   8-ounce bottle Russian, Casino, or Catalina dressing
2   envelopes onion soup mix
1   8-ounce jar apricot or peach jam

Preheat the oven to 300°. Place the chicken in a shallow greased baking pan or dish, skin side up. In a separate bowl, mix the dressing, soup mix, and jam, and spread over the chicken. Bake, covered, for 1 hour, then uncovered for 1 hour. Yield: 8 servings.

Ham Loaf

2½ pounds ground smoked ham
½   pound ground fresh pork
3   eggs, beaten
1   cup breadcrumbs
1   cup milk
¼   teaspoon pepper
1½ tablespoons prepared mustard
½   cup packed dark brown sugar
¾   cup pineapple juice

Have your butcher grind the smoked ham and pork. Preheat the oven to 350°. In a large bowl mix the meat, eggs, breadcrumbs, milk, and pepper thoroughly. Place in a shallow baking dish. Mix the mustard and brown sugar, and spread on the ham loaf. Bake for 1 hour and 30 minutes, basting several times with the pineapple juice. Yield: 8 to 10 servings.

Buffet Stroganoff

½ cup butter
2 pounds boneless sirloin, cut into 1-inch strips
1½ cups mushroom pieces
½ cup sliced green peppers
½ cup sliced onions

2 cups beef stock
1 teaspoon salt
½ teaspoon pepper
¼ cup all-purpose flour
1½ cups sour cream
Hot buttered noodles

In a saucepan heat the butter and sauté the beef until brown. Add the mushrooms, peppers, and onions. Sauté. Add the beef stock, salt, and pepper (if the beef stock is made from cubes, reduce the salt to ½ teaspoon). Simmer for 15 minutes. In a medium bowl mix the flour with the sour cream. Add to the beef mixture, stirring well to thicken. Simmer for an additional 15 minutes. Serve over hot buttered noodles. Yield: 6 to 8 servings.

Chicken Casserole

2 tablespoons butter
1½ cups chopped green onions
2 cups chopped celery
1 package herb stuffing mix
½ cup butter
1 cup water
3 cups chopped cooked chicken

½ cup mayonnaise
¾ teaspoon salt
¼ teaspoon pepper
2 eggs, beaten
1¼ cups milk
1 10¾-ounce can cream of mushroom soup

In a skillet heat 2 tablespoons butter and sauté the onion and celery. Meanwhile spread half of the herb stuffing mix in a greased 9 x 13-inch baking dish. In a saucepan heat ½ cup butter and the water and pour over the mix. In a large bowl mix the chicken, sautéed onion and celery, mayonnaise, salt, and pepper. Spread over the crumb mixture in the baking dish. Cover and refrigerate overnight.

Remove from the refrigerator 1 hour before baking. Preheat the oven to 350°. In a large bowl mix the eggs, milk, and cream of mushroom soup, and spread the soup mixture over the casserole, sprinkling the remaining herb stuffing mix on top. Bake for 1 hour. Yield: 10 to 12 servings.

Recipes from Miss Daisy's

Easy Jambalaya

½ cup butter
1 large onion, chopped
1 green pepper, chopped
2 cups chopped cooked ham
3 cups cooked shrimp
½ teaspoon salt

¼ teaspoon pepper
1 8-ounce can tomato sauce
1 3-ounce can tomato purée
½ cup dry sherry
2 cups cooked rice

Preheat the oven to 350°. Grease a 3-quart casserole. In a skillet heat the butter and sauté the onion and pepper. In a large mixing bowl blend the ham, shrimp, salt, pepper, tomato sauce, tomato purée, sherry, and rice. Bake in the prepared casserole for 40 minutes. Yield: 12 to 15 servings.

Buffet Meat Loaf

1½ pounds ground beef
1 cup herb stuffing mix
1 8-ounce can tomato sauce
1 egg, beaten

1½ teaspoons salt
½ teaspoon pepper
½ cup chopped onion
Catsup and parsley flakes

Preheat the oven to 350°. In a large bowl mix all of the ingredients. Shape in a baking dish. Bake for 1 hour. Before cutting into slices, spread the top of the meat loaf with catsup and sprinkle parsley flakes over the catsup. Yield: 6 to 8 servings.

Sweet and Sour Meatballs

1½ pounds ground round steak
¾ cup breadcrumbs
1 egg, beaten
1 small onion, chopped
½ teaspoon salt

¼ teaspoon pepper
1 8-ounce can tomato sauce
¾ cup catsup
½ cup sugar

Preheat the oven to 350°. In a large bowl combine the beef, breadcrumbs, egg, onion, salt, and pepper. Mix well. Shape into 1-inch balls and place in a single or double layer in a baking pan. Set aside. In another bowl combine the tomato sauce, catsup, and sugar. Pour over the meatballs. Bake for 1 hour and 30 minutes. Serve over noodles or in a chafing dish as an appetizer. This so easy because you do not have to fry all those meatballs. Yield: 6 servings.

Turkey Tetrazzini

½ cup butter
1 cup chopped onion
½ cup chopped green pepper
1½ cups chopped celery
1 10¾-ounce can cream of mushroom soup
1 cup grated Cheddar cheese
1 tablespoon all-purpose flour
3 cups chicken or turkey broth

3 cups chopped cooked turkey
1 2-ounce jar chopped pimientos
1 8-ounce can mushroom pieces
1 cup slivered almonds
1 pound spaghetti, cooked and drained
Salt and pepper to taste

Preheat the oven to 350°. Grease a 3-quart casserole. In a saucepan heat the butter and sauté the onion, pepper, and celery. Keep over the heat and add the soup, Cheddar cheese, and flour. Stir with a wire whisk until it boils. Add the broth. Blend. Remove from the heat. Add the turkey, pimientos, mushroom pieces, almonds, spaghetti, salt, and pepper. Bake in the prepared casserole for 30 minutes. Yield: 12 servings.

Wild Rice and Oyster Casserole

2	6-ounce packages long grain and wild rice with seasonings	3	pints standard oysters, drained (reserve liquid)
5	cups beef stock	3	cups Mushroom Sauce (see below)
½	cup butter		

Preheat the oven to 325°. Cook the rice according to the package directions, using beef stock in place of the water. When the rice is cooked, add the butter. In a pan heat the oysters just long enough for the edges to curl. Spoon half of the rice mixture into a buttered 3-quart casserole. Arrange half of the oysters on top. Repeat the layers. Spoon the mushroom sauce over all. Bake for 30 minutes. Yield: 12 servings.

Mushroom Sauce

3	tablespoons butter	1	8-ounce can mushroom pieces
¼	cup chopped onion		
3	tablespoons all-purpose flour	2	teaspoons curry powder
1	cup oyster liquid	½	cup heavy cream

In a saucepan heat the butter and sauté the onions. Add the flour. When bubbly, add the oyster liquid, stirring with a wire whisk until thickened. Add the remaining ingredients.

Carolyn's Chicken

6 strips uncooked bacon
1 cup rice
8 chicken pieces
  Garlic salt and pepper

1 10¾-ounce can cream of
  chicken soup
1 soup can water
  Oregano

Preheat the oven to 350°. Line a casserole with bacon strips.
Add 1 cup rice. Season the chicken with garlic salt and pepper
and place on the rice. In a medium bowl mix the soup with
the water. Pour over the chicken. Sprinkle lightly with
oregano, and cover with foil. Bake for 1 hour and 30 minutes.
Yield: 6 servings.

*This recipe was given to our collection by our late friend Judy
Wheeler. Judy was the original editor for* Recipes from Miss Daisy's *in
1978. She made Miss Daisy's Tearoom come alive. Thank you, Judy.*

Baked Fish with Shrimp-Parmesan Sauce

3 tablespoons butter
2 tablespoons all-purpose flour
½ teaspoon salt
1 cup milk
2 pounds white fish fillets
  (ocean perch, flounder, sole,
  etc.)

½ pound small cooked shrimp
¼ cup Parmesan cheese
  (optional)

Preheat the oven to 325°. Butter a flat baking dish. Make a
medium white sauce: in a skillet melt the butter, add the
flour, and cook until bubbly. Add the salt and milk, stirring
constantly. Remove from the heat. Layer the fish in the prepared baking dish. Spread the shrimp and white sauce over
the fish. Sprinkle with Parmesan cheese. Bake for 20 to 25
minutes. Yield: 6 servings.

Sally Lunn Bread

1	cup milk	⅓	cup sugar
½	cup vegetable shortening	2	teaspoons salt
¼	cup water	2	packages dry yeast
4	cups sifted all-purpose flour	3	eggs

In a saucepan heat the milk, shortening, and water until warm, 120°. Place the milk mixture in a large bowl and add 1⅓ cups of the flour, the sugar, salt, and yeast. Beat with an electric mixer on medium speed for 2 minutes. Gradually add ⅔ cup of the remaining flour and the eggs. Beat at high speed for 2 minutes. Add the remaining flour and beat by hand until blended. Cover. Let rise until double, about 1 hour and 30 minutes.

Grease a tube pan. Punch down the dough. Put in the prepared pan. Cover. Let rise for about 30 minutes. Bake for 40 to 50 minutes at 350°. Remove from the pan after cooling for 10 minutes. Yield: 12 to 15 servings.

Jalapeño Corn Bread

1 cup yellow cornmeal
1 cup cream-style corn
1 cup grated Cheddar cheese
½ cup vegetable oil
½ cup buttermilk
1 teaspoon baking soda

½ teaspoon salt
2 eggs, beaten
2 jalapeño peppers, chopped fine
2 tablespoons bacon drippings

Preheat the oven to 400°. In a large bowl mix the cornmeal, corn, Cheddar cheese, oil, buttermilk, baking soda, salt, eggs, and jalapeños. Put the bacon drippings into a 9 x 9-inch pan or an oven-safe skillet. Heat in the oven until the drippings cover the bottom of the pan. Pour the batter into the pan and bake for 20 to 25 minutes. Yield: 6 to 9 servings.

Pumpkin Muffins

¾ cup packed dark brown sugar
¼ cup molasses
½ cup soft butter
1 egg, beaten
1 cup pumpkin, cooked and mashed

1¾ cups all-purpose flour
1 teaspoon soda
¼ teaspoon salt
½ cup chopped pecans, dates, or raisins

Preheat the oven to 350°. In a large bowl mix the sugar, molasses, and butter until soft. Add the egg and pumpkin. Blend well. Into a separate bowl sift together the dry ingredients. Add to the batter, beating well. Fold in the pecans, dates, or raisins. Pour into muffin tins. Bake for 20 minutes. Yield: 16 muffins.

Desserts

Cheesecake Squares

¼ cup butter, melted
1 cup graham cracker crumbs
1 3-ounce package lemon
   gelatin
1 cup boiling water

1 8-ounce package cream
   cheese, softened
1 cup sugar
1 14½-ounce can evaporated
   milk, well chilled

Preheat the oven to 375°. In a small bowl mix the butter and crumbs. Pat into a 9 x 9-inch square pan. Bake for 8 minutes. Set aside. In a heatproof bowl dissolve the gelatin in the boiling water. Chill until it begins to harden. In a bowl mix the cream cheese and sugar until creamy. In a separate bowl whip the evaporated milk until it has the consistency of whipped cream. Add the cream cheese mixture and milk to the gelatin, mixing together until well blended and creamy. Pour into the crumb crust. Refrigerate for at least 1 hour before serving. Yield: 6 to 9 servings.

Chocolate Chess Pie

1½ cups sugar
2 eggs, slightly beaten
⅓ cup cocoa
¼ cup butter

½ cup evaporated milk
½ cup coconut
½ cup pecan pieces
1 unbaked 9-inch pie shell

Preheat the oven to 400°. In a large bowl mix all of the ingredients by hand and pour into the pie shell. Bake for 30 minutes. Cool and serve with vanilla ice cream or whipped cream. Yield: 6 servings.

Italian Cream Cake

½ cup butter	1 cup buttermilk
½ cup vegetable oil	2 cups all-purpose flour, sifted
2 cups sugar	1 teaspoon vanilla extract
5 eggs, separated	1 cup coconut
1 teaspoon baking soda	½ cup chopped nuts

Preheat the oven to 325°. Grease and flour a 9 x 13-inch cake pan or 3 8-inch layer pans. In a bowl mix the butter, oil, and sugar until soft. Add the egg yolks one at a time, beating after each addition. In a separate bowl stir the baking soda into the buttermilk. Add a small amount of flour to the batter using an electric mixer on medium speed, alternating with the buttermilk mixture. Add the vanilla, coconut, and pecans. In a separate bowl beat the egg whites until stiff and fold into the cake batter. Pour into the prepared pan(s). Bake for 45 minutes. Cool and ice. Yield: 12 to 15 servings.

Icing for Italian Cream Cake

8 ounces cream cheese, softened	1 teaspoon vanilla extract
½ cup butter, softened	½ cup chopped nuts
1 1-pound box confectioners' sugar	

In a mixing bowl beat the cream cheese and butter using an electric mixer. Add the sugar and vanilla. Mix well. Add nuts. Beat to mix. Spread on the cake.

French Coconut Pie

3	eggs, slightly beaten	½	cup melted butter
1½	cups sugar	1	cup coconut
1	teaspoon vanilla extract	1	unbaked 9-inch pie shell

Preheat the oven to 400°. In a large bowl mix all of the ingredients by hand. Pour into the pie shell. Bake for 15 minutes, then reduce the heat to 350° and continue baking for 20 to 45 minutes. Yield: 6 servings.

Japanese Fruit Pie

Follow the directions for French Coconut Pie, except add a 1-cup mixture of raisins, pecans, and coconut in place of the 1 cup coconut. Yield: 6 servings.

Bourbon and Chocolate Pecan Pie

1	cup sugar	2	tablespoons bourbon
¼	cup butter, melted	1	teaspoon vanilla extract
3	eggs, slightly beaten	½	cup chopped pecans
¾	cup light corn syrup	½	cup chocolate chips
¼	teaspoon salt	1	unbaked 9-inch pie shell

Preheat the oven to 375°. In a large bowl mix the sugar and butter until soft. Add the eggs, syrup, salt, bourbon, and vanilla. Mix until blended. Spread the pecans and chocolate chips in the bottom of the pie shell. Pour the filling into the shell. Bake for 40 to 50 minutes. This recipe was renamed *Miss Daisy's Jackson Pie* in 1982. Yield: 6 servings.

Lemon Icebox Pie

1   6-ounce carton whipped
    topping
1   6-ounce can frozen
    lemonade concentrate,
    thawed

1   14-ounce can sweetened
    condensed milk
1   prepared graham cracker
    crust

In a large bowl combine the topping, lemonade concentrate, and condensed milk, and beat using an electric mixer. Pour into the pie shell and chill for 1 hour before serving. Frozen limeade concentrate may be used in place of lemonade for a lime pie. Yield: 6 servings.

Smooth Dessert or Pie Filling

1   6-ounce package gelatin
    (strawberry, raspberry,
    peach, blueberry, etc.)
1   3.5-ounce package vanilla
    pudding (not instant type)

5   cups boiling water
1   6-ounce carton whipped
    topping

In a heatproof bowl dissolve the gelatin and pudding in the boiling water. Chill until it just begins to congeal; it will be shaky. In the bowl of an electric mixer beat the gelatin mixture and the whipped topping. Return to the refrigerator until serving time. Yield: 6 to 8 servings.

Pistachio Nut Cake

1 18.25-ounce package white cake mix	⅔ cup vegetable oil
1 3.5-ounce package instant pistachio pudding	1 cup club soda
4 eggs	1 cup chopped nuts (English walnuts or pecans)

Preheat the oven to 350°. Grease and flour a 9 x 13-inch pan or 3 layer pans. In a large bowl combine all of the ingredients and blend well using an electric mixer. Pour into the prepared pan(s). Bake for 40 minutes. Cool. Frost with Pistachio Frosting (see below). Refrigerate the cake when frosted. Yield: 12 servings.

Pistachio Frosting

1 9-ounce carton whipped topping	1 3.5-ounce package instant pistachio pudding
1 cup milk	

In a large bowl mix all of the ingredients using an electric mixer. Let stand for 10 minutes before spreading on the cake.

Feathery Fudge Cake

⅔ cup soft butter
1¾ cups sugar
2   eggs
.1   teaspoon vanilla extract
2½ squares baking chocolate,
    melted and cooled

2½ cups sifted cake flour
1¼ teaspoons baking soda
½   teaspoon salt
1¼ cups ice water

Preheat the oven to 350°. Grease and flour a 9 x 13-inch pan or 2 layer pans. In a large bowl mix the butter, sugar, eggs, and vanilla until soft using an electric mixer until very fluffy and light in color, about 5 minutes on high speed. Blend in the chocolate. Into a separate bowl sift together the flour, soda, and salt. Add the flour mixture to the batter alternately with the ice water, beating after each addition. Bake in the prepared pan(s) for 25 to 30 minutes. Cool and frost with Chocolate Satin Frosting (see below). Yield: 12 servings.

Chocolate Satin Frosting

3   cups confectioners' sugar
4½ tablespoons hot water
3½ squares baking chocolate,
    melted

1   egg
½   cup butter
1½ teaspoons vanilla extract

In a large bowl blend the sugar and hot water using an electric mixer. Add the remaining ingredients. Mix well.

Peanut Butter Cake

½ cup butter
1½ cups sugar
2 egg yolks, beaten well
½ cup buttermilk
1 teaspoon baking soda
½ cup water

2 heaping tablespoons peanut butter
1½ cups sifted cake flour
1 teaspoon baking powder
2 egg whites, stiffly beaten

Preheat the oven to 375°. Grease and flour a 9 x 13-inch pan or 2 round or square layer pans. In a large bowl mix the butter and sugar until soft. Add the egg yolks. In a medium bowl mix the buttermilk with the baking soda; add the water. Add the peanut butter to the butter mixture. Into a separate bowl sift together the cake flour and baking powder. Add the flour mixture and buttermilk mixture alternately to the batter, beating well after each addition. Fold in the egg whites. Bake in the prepared pan(s) for 25 to 30 minutes. Cool and frost with Peanut Butter Frosting (see below). Yield: 12 servings.

Peanut Butter Frosting

1 1-pound box confectioners' sugar
4 tablespoons vegetable shortening

4 heaping tablespoons peanut butter
½ to ¾ cup heavy cream
1 teaspoon vanilla extract

In a large bowl mix all of the ingredients well, starting with ½ cup heavy cream and adding more if needed to reach spreading consistency.

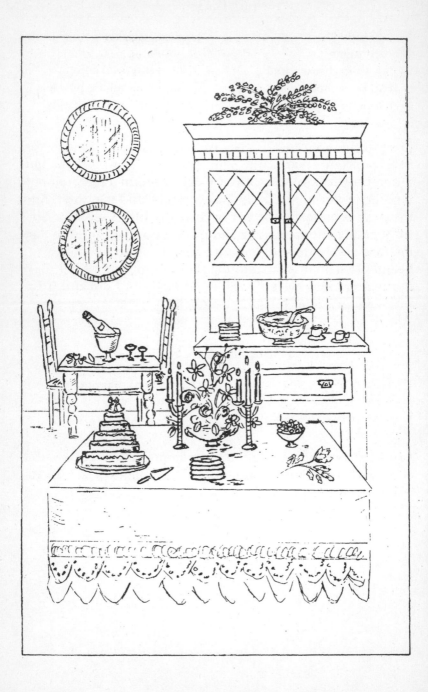

Special Days at the Restaurant

If you heard the sound of much gaiety and laughter, it was probably a "Special Day" at Miss Daisy's. The honoree might have been a national celebrity or a new bride, or a "Special Day" might have benefited a charity. It was a time for reverie and reflection, or fun and frolic. It was a time to look forward to and a time to look back upon. A special event was any event when food other than the regular menu was served.

Most modern homes are not designed to accommodate large numbers of people. So since the restaurant was once a home, it became the ideal place to entertain a large group and still maintain the warmth of an "at home" atmosphere. With masses of fresh flowers or greenery and a delectable menu, the stage was set for a wedding reception, a press reception, or whatever the imagination allowed.

One year the restaurant offered a Merry Month of May teatime. In midafternoon it became a haven for tired shoppers. Many varieties of tea were offered with crumpets. However, the specialty of the house, as always, was hospitality—Southern style.

If the guests could not stay for lunch, the lunch would go with the guests. For lack of time, many tour groups preferred to have lunch while en route to the next attraction.

Whether you liked simple foods or foods with flair, sunlight or candlelight—whether you were entertaining the president of the United States or your mother-in-law—Miss Daisy made it a special event catered to your whims.

MISS DAISY'S BOX LUNCH
Fried Chicken
Pimiento Cheese Sandwich (see p. 40)
Ham Salad in Pastry Cups
Chess Tarts
Fresh Fruit
Iced Tea

Fried Chicken

2	eggs	1	teaspoon paprika
1	cup buttermilk	8	pieces chicken, unskinned
½	teaspoon salt	2	cups all-purpose flour
½	teaspoon pepper	2	cups vegetable oil

In a large bowl beat the eggs and buttermilk with a fork, and add the salt, pepper, and paprika. Dip the chicken into the egg mixture, then dip into the flour. In a skillet with a lid heat the oil and fry the chicken. Brown on one side, turn, and brown on the other. Cover the pan and cook on low heat for 20 minutes. Yield: 8 servings.

Ham Salad

2	cups cubed cooked ham	½	cup mayonnaise
1	cup diced celery	¼	cup light cream
½	cup diced apples		Lettuce cups or pastry shells

In a large bowl combine all of the ingredients and serve in lettuce cups or pastry shells. Yield: 6 servings.

Chess Tarts

3 eggs, beaten	6 tablespoons buttermilk
1½ cups sugar	½ cup melted butter
1 teaspoon vanilla extract	6 to 8 tart shells

Preheat the oven to 350°. In a large bowl mix all of the ingredients. Pour into the tart shells and bake for 30 minutes, then reduce the oven temperature to 300° and cook for 10 more minutes until the tarts are set. Yield: 6 to 8 tarts.

UNITED STATES SENATOR'S RECEPTION

Shrimp Cucumber Rounds

Pecan Sandies

Fudge Cake Squares (see p. 86)

Orange Frost

Ham and Yeast Rolls

Bowls of Fresh Fruit with Sour Cream or Confectioners' Sugar

Platter of Assorted Cheeses

Shrimp Cucumber Rounds

20 slices whole-wheat bread
1¼ cups cream cheese, whipped
5 dozen cucumber slices

5 dozen cooked small shrimp

Using a biscuit cutter or a juice glass cut the slices of whole-wheat bread into rounds, making 3 rounds per slice. Spread each round with 1 teaspoon whipped cream cheese. Top with a slice of cucumber and a small cooked shrimp. (You may want to add a small amount of cream cheese to the top of the cucumber slice to secure the shrimp.) Yield: 5 dozen.

Pecan Sandies

2 cups butter	4 cups sifted all-purpose flour
¼ cup confectioners' sugar	2 cups chopped pecans
4 teaspoons vanilla extract	Confectioners' sugar
2 tablespoons water	

Preheat the oven to 300°. In a large bowl mix the butter and sugar until soft. Add the vanilla and stir in the water and flour. Blend well. Fold in the pecans. Form into small (1½-inch) crescents. Place on an ungreased baking sheet and bake for 20 minutes. Remove from the oven and dust with confectioners' sugar while hot. Yield: 3 dozen.

Orange Frost

3 12-ounce cans frozen orange juice, diluted	2 quarts orange sherbet
	Orange slices
8 quarts ginger ale, chilled	Sprigs of mint

Combine the orange juice and ginger ale and pour over the orange sherbet. Float slices of orange and sprigs of mint in the punch bowl for garnishes. Yield: 100 4-ounce servings.

```
┌─────────────────────────────────────────────┐
│ ┌─────────────────────────────────────────┐  │
│ │            AFTERNOON TEA                 │  │
│ │            Raisin Biscuits               │  │
│ │             Tea Cakes                    │  │
│ │             Crumpets                     │  │
│ │            Lemon Curd                    │  │
│ │            Assorted Teas                 │  │
│ └─────────────────────────────────────────┘  │
└─────────────────────────────────────────────┘
```

Raisin Biscuits

2½ cups all-purpose flour		⅓	cup shortening
1	tablespoon sugar	1	egg
1	teaspoon salt	¾	cup milk
4	teaspoons baking powder	1	cup seedless raisins

Preheat the oven to 400°. Into a large bowl sift together the flour, sugar, salt, and baking powder. Cut in the shortening. In a small bowl break the egg and beat well, then add the milk and raisins. Mix into the dough using a spoon. Turn onto a well-floured board and knead until smooth. Roll out to ½-inch thickness, and cut with a tea biscuit cutter. Bake for 10 to 12 minutes. Yield: 12 servings.

Tea Cakes

½	cup butter	½	teaspoon baking soda
½	cup shortening	2	teaspoons baking powder
2	cups sugar	½	cup buttermilk
3	eggs, beaten	1	teaspoon vanilla extract
1	cup flour, plus enough to make a soft dough		

Preheat the oven to 350°. In a large bowl mix the butter and shortening until soft. Add the sugar, then the beaten eggs. In a medium bowl place 1 cup of flour and sift the soda and baking powder. Add this to the sugar mixture. Add the milk and vanilla and enough flour to make a soft dough. Turn onto a floured board, and knead until smooth. Roll out to ¼-inch thickness. Cut into any shape. Bake for about 10 minutes or until brown. Yield: 6 dozen.

Recipes from Miss Daisy's

Crumpets

2 eggs	4 cups all-purpose flour
1 cup milk, warmed until tepid	1 teaspoon salt
1 compressed yeast cake dissolved in ½ cup water	

In a large bowl beat the eggs together well. Add the milk, yeast, flour, and salt, making a stiff batter. Let rise until light, covering the bowl to prevent crusting on top. When risen, have a griddle hot and greased. Pour a large spoonful onto the griddle carefully. Bake rather slowly, turning when one side is browned. Butter and serve with Lemon Curd. Yield: 12 to 18 servings.

Lemon Curd

5 egg yolks	1 cup sugar
1 egg white	3 tablespoons butter
¼ cup lemon juice	

In a double boiler mix all of the ingredients and cook until thick and clear, stirring constantly. Store in a jar and keep refrigerated. Serve with crumpets, tea cakes, or gingerbread, or use as a filling.

REHEARSAL DINNER

Shrimp Mold

Assorted Crackers

Tomato Juice

Baked Chicken Piquant with Rice

Green Beans with Water Chestnuts

Stuffed Squash

Rolls and Butter

Fruited Rum Ice Cream and Wedding Cookies

Coffee or Iced Tea

Shrimp Mold

1   10¾-ounce can tomato soup
1   8-ounce package cream cheese
2   envelopes plain gelatin, softened for 5 minutes in ½ cup cold water
2   pounds cooked small shrimp
¼   cup diced green onion
¼   cup diced green pepper
1   cup diced celery
¼   teaspoon each: salt, pepper, celery salt, onion salt, hot sauce
1   cup mayonnaise
2   tablespoons drained horseradish

Generously grease a 1-quart ring mold. In a saucepan heat the soup and cream cheese. Stir with a wire whisk until the cheese is melted. Some small lumps will remain. Add the dissolved gelatin. Remove from the heat and stir well. Add the remaining ingredients. Pour into the prepared mold. Refrigerate until set. Garnish as desired. Yield: 40 to 50 servings as an appetizer spread.

3 cups Burgundy wine	1 teaspoon ground ginger
1 cup soy sauce	1 teaspoon dried oregano
1 cup salad oil	¼ cup brown sugar
1 cup water	1 1-pound box long grain rice
4 cloves garlic, minced	8 chicken breast halves

Preheat the oven to 350°. In a large bowl combine the wine, soy sauce, oil, water, garlic, ginger, oregano, and brown sugar. Spread the rice in the bottom of a 9 x 13-inch baking dish. Place the chicken breasts on top of the rice. Pour the Burgundy mixture over all. Cover with foil and bake for 1 hour and 30 minutes. Add more water if the rice becomes dry during the last 30 minutes of baking. Yield: 8 servings.

Green Beans with Water Chestnuts

3   16-ounce cans whole or cut
    green beans, drained
2   10¾-ounce cans cream of
    mushroom soup
2   6-ounce cans water
    chestnuts, drained and sliced
¼   teaspoon pepper
¼   teaspoon onion salt
1   2.8-ounce can French-fried
    onion rings, crushed

Preheat the oven to 350°. Butter a 2-quart casserole. In a large bowl mix the green beans, soup, water chestnuts, pepper, and onion salt. Place in the prepared casserole. Sprinkle the crushed onion rings on top. Bake for 30 minutes. Yield: 8 to 10 servings.

Stuffed Squash

5   medium yellow squash
¼   cup butter
½   cup minced onion
¼   cup breadcrumbs
¼   cup minced celery
½   teaspoon salt
¼   teaspoon pepper
1   cup grated Cheddar cheese
    Paprika

Preheat the oven to 350°. In a large saucepan boil the squash in salted water just until tender. Cool, split lengthwise, and scoop out the pulp. In a saucepan heat the butter and sauté the onion and celery. Add the breadcrumbs, celery, salt, pepper, and pulp from the squash. Stuff the shells with this mixture, and top with the grated Cheddar cheese and paprika. Bake for 20 to 30 minutes. Yield: 6 servings.

Fruited Rum Ice Cream

½ gallon vanilla ice cream   ¼ to ½ cup dark rum
1 cup mixture of diced
  candied cherries, candied
  pineapple, chopped black
  walnuts or pecans

In a large bowl soften the ice cream. Mix in the candied fruit mixture and the rum, and return to the freezer until serving time. Yield: 6 servings.

Wedding Cookies

1 cup butter, softened   2¼ cups all-purpose flour
½ cup sifted confectioners'   ¼ teaspoon salt
  sugar, plus extra for coating   ¾ cup finely chopped pecans
  the cookies
1 teaspoon vanilla extract

Preheat the oven to 400°. In a large bowl mix the butter, sugar, and vanilla thoroughly. In a separate bowl blend the flour and salt, and stir into the butter mixture. Mix in the pecans. Roll into 1-inch balls. Place on an ungreased baking sheet. Bake for 10 to 12 minutes. While still warm, roll in sifted confectioners' sugar. Cool. Roll in sugar again. Yield: 6 servings.

```
┌─────────────────────────────────────────────────┐
│  ┌───────────────────────────────────────────┐  │
│  │             WEDDING RECEPTION             │  │
│  │  Marinated Artichoke Hearts, Shrimp, and Mushrooms │  │
│  │         Hot Sausage Cheese Balls          │  │
│  │   Cherry Tomatoes Filled with Chicken Salad   │  │
│  │  Sliced Smoked Turkey, Roast Beef, Ham, Cheese  │  │
│  │     Breads and Spreads for Sandwiches     │  │
│  │          Asparagus Sandwiches             │  │
│  │            Seafood Casserole              │  │
│  │   Cream Cheese and Roquefort Mold with    │  │
│  │  Assorted Fresh Fruit Cuts and Crackers   │  │
│  │             Wedding Cake                  │  │
│  │               Coffee                      │  │
│  │               Punch                       │  │
│  │             Champagne                     │  │
│  └───────────────────────────────────────────┘  │
└─────────────────────────────────────────────────┘
```

Marinated Artichoke Hearts, Shrimp, and Mushrooms

2   14-ounce cans tiny artichoke
    hearts, drained
2   4-ounce cans whole button
    mushrooms, drained

2   pounds cooked shrimp
2   packages Italian dressing
    mix

In a large bowl combine the artichoke hearts, mushrooms, and shrimp. Prepare the dressing according to the package directions. Pour dressing over all and marinate for 8 hours. Yield: 6 servings.

Hot Sausage Cheese Balls

1   pound sausage, hot or mild
1   pound extra-sharp Cheddar
    cheese, grated

3   cups biscuit mix

Preheat the oven to 350°. In a large bowl mix all of the ingredients well. Drop by teaspoonfuls onto an ungreased baking sheet. Bake for 15 to 20 minutes. Serve hot. Yield: 12 to 18 servings.

Chicken Salad

1 large hen or 4 whole breasts
1 cup diced celery
½ cup diced sweet pickle
1 cup finely chopped pecans

1 to 1½ cups mayonnaise
Pepper, celery salt, and
onion salt to taste

In a large saucepan boil the chicken in salted water until the meat begins to fall off the bones. Cool. Remove the skin and bones. Cut the chicken with scissors into small pieces and place in a large bowl. Add the celery, sweet pickle, and pecans. Mix. Add the mayonnaise to desired consistency, and season to taste. For variety you may want to add fresh white grapes, chopped apple, or fresh pineapple bits. Finely chopped toasted almonds may be substituted for the pecans. Yield: 6 to 8 lunch servings or 24 to 36 canapes.

Asparagus Sandwiches

1 loaf bread, light whole-grain variety	1 14-ounce can asparagus spears, drained
½ cup softened butter	¼ cup melted butter
1 cup Parmesan cheese	Paprika

Preheat the oven to 400°. Cut the crusts from the bread slices. Spread each slice with softened butter and sprinkle with Parmesan cheese. Roll each asparagus spear diagonally in a piece of bread. Secure with toothpicks. Before baking brush each roll with melted butter and sprinkle with the remaining Parmesan cheese and some paprika. Bake for 10 to 12 minutes. Yield: 14 servings.

Seafood Casserole

¾ cup butter	½ teaspoon salt
½ pound mushrooms, chopped	¼ teaspoon pepper
1 cup diced cooked lobster	2 cups milk
1 cup crabmeat	2 tablespoons sherry
2 cups cooked shrimp	1 cup grated American cheese
¼ cup all-purpose flour	

Preheat the oven to 350°. Grease a 9 x 13-inch baking dish. In a skillet heat ½ cup butter and sauté the mushrooms. Add the seafood. Make a medium white sauce: in a saucepan melt ¼ cup butter, add the flour, and cook until bubbly. Add the salt and pepper, and remove from the heat. Add the milk, and bring to a boil, stirring constantly. Add the white sauce and sherry to the seafood mixture. Mix well. Pour into the prepared baking dish. Top with the American cheese. Bake for 20 to 30 minutes. Yield: 8 to 10 servings.

Cream Cheese and Roquefort Mold

2 envelopes plain gelatin, softened for 5 minutes in ½ cup cold water

1 8-ounce package cream cheese, softened

1 1½-ounce package Roquefort cheese

½ teaspoon salt

1 cup heavy cream, whipped

1 cup chopped walnuts, optional

Watercress, mint, or parsley for garnish

Grease a 1-quart mold. Set aside. In a saucepan heat the softened gelatin until dissolved. In a large bowl mix the cream cheese and Roquefort cheese using an electric mixer. Add the gelatin, salt, and whipped cream. Beat until blended. Fold in the walnuts, if desired. Pour into a greased 1-quart mold. Chill until set. Unmold, and garnish with watercress, mint, or parsley and serve with fresh fruit cuts and wheat crackers. Yield: 6 servings.

Wedding Punch

3 gallons vanilla ice cream
Yellow food coloring (optional)

3 12-ounce cans frozen orange juice concentrate, thawed

1 12-ounce can frozen limeade concentrate, thawed

3 46-ounce cans pineapple juice

1 46-ounce can apricot nectar

3 liters lemon-flavored soft drink

2 liters ginger ale

In a large bowl mash the ice cream with a potato masher or mix with an electric mixer. Add food coloring if desired. Mix the fruit juices together, and add to the softened ice cream. Add the lemon-flavored soft drink. Just before serving, add the ginger ale. Float an ice ring on top. Yield: 50 4-ounce servings.

To make an ice ring: Mash ½ gallon vanilla ice cream with a potato masher or mix with an electric mixer. Add 2 liters lemon-flavored soft drink and yellow food coloring if desired. Pour into a ring mold and freeze.

```
┌─────────────────────────────────────────────────────────┐
│                                                           │
│           FRENCH PICNIC IN COURTYARD                      │
│        Marinated Roast Filet of Beef in Brioche           │
│                 Chive Potato Salad                        │
│              Assorted Fruits and Cheeses                  │
│                 French Rum Cake                           │
│                                                           │
└─────────────────────────────────────────────────────────┘
```

Marinated Roast Filet of Beef

1 filet of beef, 5 to 6 pounds, trimmed	1 cup soy sauce
4 to 5 garlic cloves	½ cup olive oil
1 teaspoon salt	1 cup port wine
1 teaspoon freshly ground black pepper	1 teaspoon thyme
½ teaspoon hot sauce	1 bay leaf
	Bacon strips

Make small gashes in the roast and fill with garlic cloves cut into thin slivers. Rub the roast well with the salt, pepper, and hot sauce. Marinate overnight in the soy sauce, olive oil, port wine, and herbs, turning several times.

Preheat the oven to 425°. Place the roast on a rack in a shallow roasting pan and top with a few strips of bacon. Roast in the oven for 45 minutes, basting several times with the marinade. A meat thermometer inserted into the heaviest part of the roast should register 125° for rare and 140° to 150° for medium. Cool and slice paper thin for sandwiches. Yield: 15 to 18 servings.

2	packages or cakes yeast	1½	teaspoon salt
½	cup lukewarm water	7	eggs
4	cups all-purpose flour	10	ounces creamed butter
1	tablespoon sugar		

In a bowl dissolve the yeast in warm water and add 1 cup flour. Turn out, knead into a ball, slash the top criss-cross with a knife, and drop into the lukewarm water. Leave until the dough rises to the top (less than a minute). In a large bowl blend the rest of the flour with the sugar and salt, and beat in the whole eggs. Continue stirring until the mixture is smooth, and slowly add the butter. When the dough is smooth, add the drained yeast sponge. Mix in well. Cover with plastic wrap and a cloth. Set in warm spot to rise until double in bulk. Punch down the dough. Refrigerate the dough until you are ready to bake. (More a necessity than you might imagine—all that butter gets too warm and when you punch down the risen dough, you have a pool!)

When you are ready to use the dough, turn it out onto a floured board and shape into a loaf, or for individual brioches use small fluted molds or large muffin pans. Shape the dough into balls just large enough to half fill the molds. Cut a cross in each ball and insert a small ball of dough to make the head or crown of the brioche. Cover the brioches and let them rise in a warm place for about 30 minutes.

Brush them with egg white and water. Bake at 425° for about 15 minutes.

Chive Potato Salad

½ cup mayonnaise
1 teaspoon salt
½ teaspoon pepper
2 teaspoons Dijon mustard

¼ cup chopped fresh chives
2 pounds new potatoes, cooked, peeled, and sliced

In a large bowl mix the mayonnaise, salt, pepper, Dijon mustard, and chives. Toss with the cooked, peeled, and sliced potatoes. Yield: 4 servings.

French Rum Cake

¼ teaspoon salt	1 cup strong coffee
1 cup sugar	⅛ cup rum
1 teaspoon rum flavoring	Rum Cream Filling (see below)
2 eggs, beaten until thick and light	Whipped cream
½ cup milk	Drained apricot preserves
1 tablespoon butter	
1 cup all-purpose flour	
1 teaspoon baking powder	
1 cup sugar	

Preheat the oven to 350°. Grease and flour a 9-inch cake pan. In a large bowl add the salt, 1 cup sugar, and rum flavoring to the eggs; beat in. In a saucepan heat the milk and butter to boiling. Beat into the egg mixture. Into a separate bowl sift the flour and baking powder. Beat into the egg mixture. Turn into the prepared pan. Bake for 35 to 40 minutes. Prepare coffee rum syrup: in a saucepan dissolve 1 cup sugar in the coffee. Bring to a boil and boil for 3 minutes. Cool and add the rum. Spoon the syrup slowly over the entire surface of the warm cake until absorbed. Let stand until cold. Slit the cake carefully into 2 layers. Fill with Rum Cream Filling. Garnish the top with whipped cream and apricot preserves. Yield: 12 servings.

Rum Cream Filling

½ cup sugar	2 egg yolks, beaten, or 1 egg, beaten
¼ cup all-purpose flour	2 tablespoons rum
⅛ teaspoon salt	
1 cup milk	

In a double boiler combine the sugar, flour, and salt. Add the milk. Stir over low heat until thick. Cook over hot water, covered, for 10 minutes. Add a small amount of the hot mixture to the egg yolks. Combine with the remaining hot mixture. Cook for 2 minutes, stirring constantly. Chill and add rum. Yield: 8 servings.

Crab Salad in Avocado Halves

2 large avocados, cut
   lengthwise
   Bottled French dressing
1 5-ounce can crabmeat

½ cup mayonnaise
1 cup minced celery
   Russian Salad Dressing (see
   below)

Peel the avocados, and place in a bowl. Cover with French dressing to marinate. Drain. In a medium bowl combine the crabmeat with the mayonnaise and celery. Fill the avocados with the crabmeat mixture. Serve with Russian Salad Dressing. Yield: 4 servings.

Russian Salad Dressing

2 cups mayonnaise
½ cup minced onion
⅓ cup minced green pepper
1 cup finely chopped celery

½ cup sliced green olives
1 tablespoon Worcestershire
   sauce
½ cup chili sauce

In a large bowl combine all of the ingredients. Transfer to a jar or bottle, and keep refrigerated.

Molded Grapefruit Pineapple Salad

1   3-ounce package lemon
    gelatin
1   cup hot water
    Juice from pineapple
1   14-ounce can crushed
    pineapple, drained

Sections from a grapefruit
½   cup diced celery
½   cup sliced almonds

In a bowl dissolve the gelatin in the hot water. In a measuring cup add enough cold water to the juice to make 1 cup. Add to the gelatin. When almost congealed, add the crushed pineapple, grapefruit sections, celery, and almonds. Congeal in molds.

Almond Sheet Dessert

1   cup butter
1   1-pound box confectioners'
    sugar
2   tablespoons almond extract

2   cups graham cracker crumbs
½   cup shaved almonds, toasted

In a large bowl mix the butter and sugar until soft. Add the almond extract, 1 cup cracker crumbs, and the toasted almonds. Mix well. Roll out on a cookie sheet in a thin layer (not more than ½ inch thick). Refrigerate until ready to use. When ready to serve, cut into 2-inch squares, top with a scoop of vanilla ice cream, and sprinkle with the remaining crumbs. A pretty party dessert. Yield: 18 to 24 servings.

PRESS BRUNCH
Egg Casserole
Sausage Balls in Apple Butter
Garlic Cheese Grits
Hot Fruit Compote
Sour Cream Coffee Cake
Buttermilk Banana Bread (see p. 72)
Coffee or Hot Spiced Tea

Egg Casserole

9 hard-boiled eggs
1 pound bacon, sautéed
3 cups White Sauce (see below)

2 cups grated cheese
   Breadcrumbs

Preheat the oven to 350°. Grate the eggs and crumble the bacon. Alternate layers of White Sauce, eggs, bacon, and cheese to fill a 2-quart casserole. Add extra white sauce and breadcrumbs to the top. Bake for 30 minutes. Yield: 9 to 12 servings.

White Sauce

2 tablespoons butter
1 tablespoon all-purpose flour
1 teaspoon salt
1 teaspoon pepper

1 teaspoon Worcestershire sauce
1 to 1½ cups light cream or milk

In saucepan melt the butter. Stir in the flour, salt, pepper, and Worcestershire sauce. Gradually add the light cream or milk, and cook over medium heat until creamy or of consistency desired. *Note:* For the Egg Casserole, you will need to triple this recipe. Yield: 1 cup.

Recipes from Miss Daisy's

Sausage Balls in Apple Butter

1 pound mild sausage	1 16 to 20-ounce jar apple butter

Make marble-sized sausage balls. Sauté in a skillet until cooked. Drain on a paper towel. When ready to serve, heat the apple butter in a saucepan or chafing dish and add the sausage balls. Keep warm while serving. Yield: 5 dozen.

Garlic Cheese Grits

1¼ cups grits, uncooked	2 eggs
3½ cups boiling water	1 cup milk
1 roll garlic cheese	½ cup grated Cheddar cheese
½ cup butter	

Preheat the oven to 350°. Grease a 2-quart casserole. In a saucepan cook the grits in boiling water for about 30 minutes or until done. Crumble the garlic cheese and butter into the cooked grits. In a medium bowl blend the eggs and milk together. Mix the egg mixture with the grits. Pour into the prepared casserole and bake for 45 minutes, uncovered. Sprinkle with the Cheddar cheese and bake for 15 minutes more until the cheese is melted. Yield: 6 to 8 servings.

Hot Fruit Compote

1	16-ounce can pear halves	12	maraschino cherries
1	16-ounce can sliced peaches	¾	cup light brown sugar
1	16-ounce can pineapple chunks	3	teaspoons curry powder
		⅓	cup melted butter
1	16-ounce can apricot halves	⅔	cup slivered almonds

Preheat the oven to 325°. Drain the fruit. In a small bowl add the sugar and curry powder to the melted butter. Arrange the fruit and nuts in layers in a 2-quart casserole. Pour the butter mixture over all and bake for 1 hour. Refrigerate overnight.

Reheat at 350° before serving. Be sure to prepare this a day ahead of time. Yield: 10 to 12 servings.

Sour Cream Coffee Cake

1	cup sour cream	1	cup butter
¾	teaspoon baking soda	1	cup sugar
½	cup packed dark brown sugar	2	eggs
		1	teaspoon vanilla extract
½	cup chopped pecans	1½	cups all-purpose flour, sifted
1	teaspoon cinnamon	1½	teaspoons baking powder

In a small bowl mix the sour cream and soda and let stand for 1 hour.

Preheat the oven to 350°. Grease and flour a tube pan. In a small bowl mix the brown sugar, pecans, and cinnamon for the topping. In a large bowl mix the butter and sugar until soft. Add the eggs and vanilla, and beat. Add the sour cream mixture. Stir in the sifted flour and baking powder. Beat until smooth. Alternate layers of batter and topping in the prepared pan, starting with the batter and ending with the topping. Bake for 40 minutes. Cool in the pan for 15 minutes, then remove. Yield: 12 servings.

Recipes from Miss Daisy's

INDEX

Appetizers

Asparagus Sandwiches, 131
Black-Eyed Susans, 48
Cheese Ball, 48
Cheese Straws, 49
Chili Con Queso, 46
Crab Dip Divine, 46
Cream Cheese and Roquefort Mold, 135
Cucumber Ball, 49
Curry Dip, 47
Guacamole Dip, 47
Hot Broccoli Dip, 46
Hot French Cheese Sandwiches, 18
Hot Sausage Cheese Balls, 132
Marinated Artichoke Hearts, Shrimp, and
    Mushrooms, 132
Marinated Mushrooms, 50
Miss Daisy's Pimiento Cheese Sandwich Filling, 40
Nuts and Bolts, 51
Peppery Spiced Nuts, 52
Poppy Seed Squares, 49
Sausage Balls in Apple Butter, 143
Shrimp Cucumber Rounds, 124
Shrimp Dip, 47
Smoked Turkey Fingers, 52
Sour Cream and Onion Dip, 48
Stuffed Mushrooms, 50
Toasted Mushroom Rolls, 51

Beverages

Coca-Cola Punch, 53
Cran-Orange Punch, 54
Hot Chocolate Mix, 53

Hot Cranberry Tea, 54
Hot Spiced Apple Cider, 53
Hot Spiced Tea, 54
Hot V-8, 55
Orange Frost, 125
Sangria, 55
Tea Punch, 40
Wedding Punch, 135

Breads

Angel Biscuits, 72
Bran Muffins, 9
Brioche, 137
Buttermilk Banana Bread, 72
Cheese Drop Biscuits, 73
Chocolate Date Bread, 73
Corn Light Bread, 74
Cornmeal Muffin Rings, 14
Cranberry Tea bread, 75
Crunchy Cheese Biscuits, 29
Fudge Muffins, 76
Jalapeño Corn Bread, 112
Lemon Muffins, 75
Parmesan Cheese Biscuits, 74
Pineapple Surprise, 77
Pumpkin Bread, 25
Pumpkin Muffins, 112
Quick Light Bread, 74
Raisin Biscuits, 126
Refrigerator Potato Rolls, 77
Sally Lunn Muffins, 11
Spoon Rolls, 33
Toasted Cheese Muffins, 17
Tropical Muffins, 76
Sally Lunn Bread, 111

Desserts, Cakes

Almond Sheet Dessert, 141
Angel Cake—Chocolate Sauce, 84
Apricot Nectar Cake, 38
Banana Pineapple Cake, 93
Cheesecake Squares, 113
Chess Cake, 31
Chocolate Cookie Sheet Cake, 83
Dump Cake, 42
Feathery Fudge Cake, 118

Recipes from Miss Daisy's

Miss Daisy's Five Flavor Pound Cake, 34
French Rum Cake, 139
Fresh Apple Cake, 81
Fresh Carrot Cake with Cream Cheese
    Frosting, 27
Fudge Cake, 86
Heath Bar Cake, 11
Italian Cream Cake, 114
Kentucky Butter Cake, 82
Lemon Supreme Cake, 25
Orange Pound Cake, 86
Peanut Butter Cake, 119
Pistachio Nut Cake, 117
Poppy Seed Cake, 17
Pound Cake, 85
Pumpkin Squares with Cream Cheese
    Frosting, 43
Rum Cake, 85
Skillet Coffee Cake, 84
Sour Cream Coffee Cake, 144
Sour Cream Pound Cake, 20
Springtime Torte, 93
Strawberry Angel Food Cake, 87
Tangy Citrus Cake, 29

Desserts, Pies

Bourbon and Chocolate Pecan Pie, 115
Buttermilk Pie, 9
Buttermilk Raisin Pie, 89
Chess Pie, 40
Chess Tarts, 123
Chocolate Chess Pie, 113
Chocolate Chip-Almond Pie, 87
Chocolate Tarts, 78
Coconut Icebox Pie, 91
Cornmeal Pie, 91
French Coconut Pie, 115
Fudge Pie, 15
Grasshopper Pie and Chocolate Wafer Crust, 88
Japanese Fruit Pie, 115
Lemon Icebox Pie, 116
Macaroon Pie, 92
Millionaire Pie, 89
Peach Cobbler, 80
Peanut Butter Ice Cream Pie, 88
Pecan Pie, 19
Rum Cream Pie, 90

Apple Crisp, 78
Crème de Menthe Party Dessert, 79
Crumpets, 127
Fat Man's Misery, 79
Flowerpot Dessert, 23
Fruited Rum Ice Cream, 131
Hello Dollies, 80
Hot Fruit Crisp, 21
Ice Cream Pecan Ball with Butterscotch
    Sauce, 13
Lemon Curd, 127
Lemon Freeze, 36
Lemon Squares, 81
Pecan Sandies, 125
Smooth Dessert or Pie Filling, 116
Tea Cakes, 126
Wedding Cookies, 131

Entrees

Baked Chicken Piquant with Rice, 129
Baked Fish with Shrimp-Parmesan Sauce, 110
Beef Burgundy, 65
Brunswick Stew, 71
Buffet Meat Loaf, 107
Buffet Stroganoff, 106
Carolyn's Chicken, 110
Cheese Soufflé, 41
Chicken Breasts in Wine, 65
Chicken Casserole, 106
Corn and Ham Chowder, 21
Creamed Chicken, 14
Creole Pork Chops, 67
Easy Jambalaya, 107
Egg Casserole, 142
French Pot Roast, 67
Fried Chicken, 122
Ham Casserole, 66
Ham Loaf, 105
Hot Baked Chicken Salad, 66
Hot Tuna Sandwich with Mushroom Cheese Sauce, 35
Marinated Roast Filet of Beef, 136
Melange of Chipped Beef and Mushrooms over
    Chinese Noodles, 32
Mexican Casserole, 22

Miss Daisy's Beef Casserole, 26
Parmesan Round Steak, 69
Quiche Lorraine, 37
Sausage Casserole, 69
Seafood and Rice Casserole, 70
Shrimp Creole, 10
Split Pea Soup with Sherry, 43
Steak Oriental, 68
Sweet and Sour Chicken, 105
Sweet and Sour Meatballs, 108
Tearoom Chili, 20
Tuna Cashew Casserole, 68
Turkey Divan, 8
Turkey Tetrazzini, 108
Veal Parmesan, 70
Welsh Rabbit, 30
Wild Rice and Oyster Casserole, 109

Salads

Apricot Salad, 56
Bing Cherry Salad, 56
Black-Eyed Pea Salad—Greek Style, 57
Carter's Court Salad Bowl, 12
Chicken Salad, 133
Chive Potato Salad, 138
Christmas Ribbon Salad, 97
Congealed Beet Salad, 32
Congealed Cucumber Salad, 10
Congealed Green Pea Salad, 57
Congealed Spiced Peach Salad, 9+
Corn Relish, 36
Crab Salad in Avocado Halves, 140
Festive Cranberry Salad, 15
Festive Shrimp Salad with Sour Cream
    Dressing, 28
Fresh Fruit Bowl, 24
Frozen Cherry Salad, 8
Garden Tomato Stuffed with Tearoom Tuna Salad, 18
Grandmother Hubbard's Frozen Fruit Salad, 39
Ham Salad, 122
Honey-French Dressing, 12
Hot Fruit Compote,
Lime Fluff, 97
Marinated Carrots,
Marinated Green Vegetables, 98
Molded Grapefruit Pineapple Salad, 140

Orange Sherbet Salad, 58
Party Salad Topping, 59
Peppermint Stick Candy Salad, 58
Pineapple Salad Supreme, 57
Pink Arctic Freeze, 41
Poppy Seed Dressing, 24
Russian Salad Dressing, 140
Sauerkraut Salad, 98
Seven-Cup Salad, 58
Shrimp Aspic Mold with Horseradish
    Dressing, 16
Shrimp Mold, 128
Strawberry-Lemon Congealed Salad, 96
Summer Salad, 59
Tomato Aspic, 28
Tuna Mousse, 99
Waldorf Salad, 30

Vegetables

Asparagus and English Pea Casserole, 100
Baked Limas with Sour Cream, 61
Best Baked Beans, 60
Broccoli with Horseradish Dressing, 61
Broccoli-Rice Casserole, 100
Carrot-Raisin Casserole, 104
Corn Pudding, 103
Easy Spinach Casserole, 102
Eggplant Casserole, 103
Eggplant Soufflé, 62
Garlic Cheese Grits,
Green Bean Casserole, 60
Green Beans with Water Chestnuts, 130
Herbed Tomatoes, 64
Onion Casserole, 62
Oriental Vegetable Casserole, 102
Party Squash, 62
Quick and Easy Peas, 104
Rice Supreme, 101
Spinach and Artichoke Casserole, 63
Spinach and Tomato Bake, 101
Stuffed Squash, 130
Squash Casserole, 104
Sweet Potato Pudding, 102
Sweet Potatoes in Orange Cups, 64
Vegetable Casserole, 63

GIFT ORDER BLANK

Recipes from Miss Daisy's
P.O. Box 864
Franklin, Tennessee 37065

Please send _____ copies of Recipes from Miss Daisy's at
$12.00 per copy to friends whose names and addresses are
listed below. Enclosed is my check or money order for
$_____. Make the check payable to *Recipes from Miss Daisy's*
and mail to the above address.

My name _____

Street address _____

City, state, and ZIP _____

....

Send cookbooks to:

Name _____

Street address _____

City, state, and ZIP _____

Name _____

Street address _____

City, state, and ZIP _____

Name _____

Street address _____

City, state, and ZIP _____

Name _____

Street address _____

City, state, and ZIP _____